Explore a Castle

EXPLORE A CASTLE

BRIAN DAVISON

Hamish Hamilton · London

Thank You

I should like to say 'thank you' to all the people who helped me when I was writing this book.

In particular, I should like to thank the children and staff of Lindfield Junior School in Sussex. They read early versions of each chapter and made helpful suggestions as to how the book could be made better. Without their help I would not have been able to write the book.

I should also like to thank Jason Corbally and Sharon Doyle for letting themselves be photographed for the cover of the book.

Finally, I should like to thank my three daughters, Roisin, Grainne and Fionnuala, for all their help and encouragement – even if some of their comments were less than polite!

Brian Davison

Acknowledgments

The author and publishers would like to thank the following for permission to use their photographs: British Tourist Authority, 10; Crown Copyright – the Controller of HMSO, 2, 3, 12, 24, 28, 29, 32, 34, 90, 91, 95; Crown Copyright – the Scottish Development Department, 36, 38; Welsh Office, 33; Chris Fairclough, 14; National Monuments Record, 92, 94; R. H. Windsor, 21.

Illustrations by Bill le Fever
Design by Don Macpherson
Cover photographs by Chris Fairclough

First published 1982 by
Hamish Hamilton Children's Books
Garden House, 57–59 Long Acre, London WC2E 9JZ
© 1982 Brian Davison
All rights reserved

Printed in Great Britain by Thomson Litho Ltd, East Kilbride, Scotland

Contents

Introduction

When you first saw a castle, was it exciting and romantic, with flags flying above the battlements? Or were you a bit disappointed? Did you think to yourself: 'Why, it's just a ruin! It's a heap of old stones!'

Some castles are still lived in. They are kept well repaired. There are roofs on the towers and glass in the windows. There may be lilies growing in the moat. Such castles are rare. Most castles stopped being lived in many hundreds of years ago and are now ruins. They don't look the same as the brightly-coloured pictures of castles you find in books. This is because the people who drew those pictures had to use their imagination to put into the picture all those things which were missing from the real castle – the flags, the drawbridges, and especially the people.

Ruins can be fun, however. After all, providing you don't carve your name on the walls, there isn't much you can do to harm a castle. It was built to take rough treatment. You can run, jump, hide and explore in a way that you can't in a castle or old house that is still lived in. This book is about exploring a castle, using your imagination to become a Castle Detective.

One of the best things about castles is that there are such a lot of them. Even though there may not be one in your own town or village, the chances are that there is one not too far away. Almost certainly there will be one near enough to visit during a day out with your school class, your parents or your friends. There are more than a thousand castles in England, Wales, Scotland and Ireland. Some of them are listed at the end of this book, but there are many, many more. Finding them unexpectedly when you are looking for something else is part of the fun.

Because castles were built for different purposes, and because they remained in fashion for such a long time, there are many different kinds of castle. All of them have some features in common. They all have battlements, for example, and almost all have towers set along the walls. But the plan of the castle, the shape of the towers, the number of buildings inside the castle – these can be very different. No two castles are exactly the same.

Some castles were built by the king, to guard a ford or protect a town. They provided a centre for his soldiers and were a home for him

Dover Castle, Kent: A royal fortress, built to guard the kingdom against invasion.

when he was in that part of the country. Others were built by his barons, to protect the lands the king had given them. Each man had a different idea of what was best. Each needed a castle for a different purpose. When the lord of the castle died, his son would inherit his castle. He might want to use it in a different way. He might knock down some parts of it and add new buildings where he thought they were needed.

Some men were rich and built huge castles. Others were not so rich and were content with much smaller castles. This variety of size and shape and purpose means that castles never get boring. Each new castle you find will have something different about it, something new to discover, some puzzle to solve – if you can find the clues.

Castles were first built in this country at the time of the Norman Conquest in 1066. Men were still building castles four hundred years later. By then, castles looked very different from those built when the Normans first came to Britain. Four hundred years is hard to imagine! Think of yourself and your grandparents. Your Granny and Grandpa were probably born some time about 1920; that is, just over sixty years

Eynesford Castle, Kent: The private castle of a Norman knight, built to protect his home against attack.

4   ago. If you ask them, they will tell you about the things that have changed since they were your age. Some things have changed a lot. There weren't so many cars and aeroplanes then. Some people still used horses to plough the fields and to pull carts. Buildings weren't as high as they are now: there were no tall blocks of flats. Towns and villages were smaller, slower and quieter than today.

     That was only sixty years ago. Ask your grandparents what *their* grandparents told them life was like when *they* were young, a hundred and twenty years ago. A lot more things have changed since then!

Time Chart

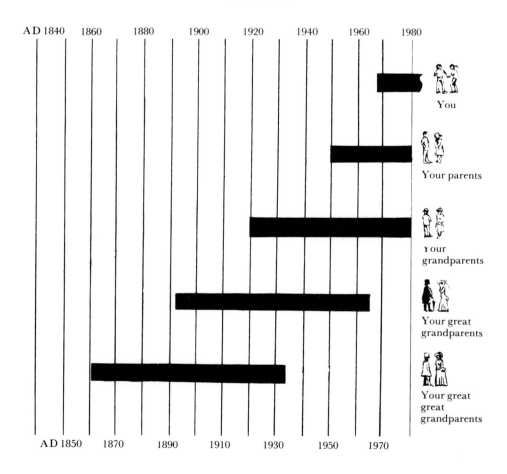

In the Middle Ages things didn't change quite so quickly as they do nowadays. Even so, great changes did take place in the four hundred years between the building of the first and last castles. Battles and sieges led to armour and weapons being improved. Castles were built in new ways so as to be more easily defended against the new weapons. The shapes of towers and arrow-slits, drawbridges and gateways changed from century to century. Not only did the shape of castles change. The habits of their owners changed too. Kings and barons began to lead more complicated lives. They demanded more and more comfort in their castles. After all, the castles were their homes. They wanted more windows and fireplaces, better kitchens and toilets, more room for guests. By the end of the Middle Ages builders had to provide much more elaborate castles than at the time of the Norman Conquest.

Castles thus differ from each other according to *why* they were built and also *when* they were built. They may be large and rambling, set on the top of a hill where everyone can see them; or they may be small and compact, set within a moat in the bottom of a valley. They may be well preserved or completely ruined. All of them are fun!

The purpose of this book is to help you find out just when a castle was built, why it was built, and what it was like to live in. If you use your imagination and the clues provided in this book, you can be a Castle Detective.

The chapters follow the way in which you visit a castle. At the end of each chapter you will find a check list which you can use to help you find out what you want to know. You don't have to use these check lists, but if you want to try being a detective they will help.

In Chapter 1, as you walk from the car park towards the castle, you will be wondering what sort of person built the castle. Why did he choose to build it here rather than somewhere else? How long did it take to build? How much did it cost? The clues are in Chapter 1. Chapter 2 is for when you have got up close to the castle. Don't rush inside at once. Walk around the outside, looking at it. Does its shape tell you how old it is? Was it all built at once, or was it built piece by piece over a long time? When you get inside, Chapter 3 will help you find out how the castle was defended. How many soldiers were needed? What weapons would they have had? What could the enemy do to capture the castle? How long could the defenders hold on before their supplies of food ran out and they were forced to surrender?

Life in a castle was not always dangerous. Most castles were attacked only very occasionally. Some were never attacked at all. Chapter 4 tells you how people lived in castles in peace-time. Where did the lord of the castle live? Where did his guests stay? Where were the servants' quarters? Was there a chapel? Where was the prison or dungeon? How comfortable was it to live in a castle? What did the children do? Finally, as you walk back to the car park, there is the question of why it all came to an end. Why did the people go away and leave the castle to fall down?

At the back of the book is a map and a list of castles to visit. These are just a start: there are many more castles than can be listed here. There is also a glossary explaining what some of the special words used in this book mean, and an index so that you can quickly look up something if you need to. If you like making models, you can follow the instructions at the back of the book and make your own model castle. You will find all the pieces are interchangeable so you can make your castle as large or as small as you like. You can have all the towers the same shape or you can mix them, designing your own castle to be both a strong fortress and a comfortable home.

This book is one half of a team. You are the other half. You are going to be the expert, using your eyes to find the clues hidden in the ruins. You are the Castle Detective.

Chapter 1
Why is it there?

Castles were built to protect knights.

A knight was a warrior, trained to fight on horseback. He was equipped with expensive armour and weapons. His horse was expensive too. It had to be larger and stronger than most other horses, so that it could carry the extra weight of the knight's armour. It had to be specially trained to carry him into battle and not be frightened by the noise or by the smell of blood. The knight and his horse were the backbone of the army in the Middle Ages. They were rather like the tanks of modern armies – heavy, fast-moving and powerful. However, there were times when both man and horse had to rest. Then a safe place was needed where the knight could dismount and take off his armour, and where the horse could be stabled. To be really safe, such places had to have strong walls. This is what we mean by the word *castle*.

In the Middle Ages there was no full-time army like today's army. Knights enjoyed fighting and spent much of their time practising: even their tournaments were practice fights. Often, however, there were long periods of peace when a knight could relax. He could hunt deer or go hawking; he could stay at home, and play chess or listen to music. Yet even when he was off-duty, there were many things to be done. A knight might have to act as the king's representative. He might have to hold a court and sentence wrong-doers, lock up prisoners, or look after money and valuables. His castle was therefore not only his safe place: it was also a courthouse, a jail and a bank. Above all, it was his home. It was where he lived with his family.

Not all knights were the same. Some were rich, some were poor. The king was a knight. He had been trained to fight on horseback and was expected to lead his army into battle. Although he was rather like a modern general, he had to fight in exactly the same way as the other knights, with sword and shield and spear. It was this shared duty that bound the king and his knights together. They were the fighting men of the army.

Some knights were paid to fight. But most knights fought for the king because he had given them their homes. In the Middle Ages all land belonged to the king. He didn't need all of it and so he gave parts of it (called *fiefs*) to his most trusted friends, asking in return that each of them should serve him faithfully. In particular, each man was to come to the king's aid when called, bringing with him a certain number of other knights. In this way an army could be assembled whenever necessary. These friends of the king – the richest and most powerful men after the king himself – were called *barons*. They kept some of the land the king had given them and gave the rest to other knights. The barons asked that each of these knights should serve them faithfully and ride with them to serve the king when he requested it.

In this way, poorer or humbler knights served their lord, the baron, and the baron in his turn served *his* lord, the king. Each had his place in society, each had his own duties to carry out. What united

King Henry

Earl Hugh   Lord John   William the Marshal   Earl Stephen

Hugh's Knights   John's Knights   William's Knights   Stephen's Knights

10   them, and set tnem apart from the merchants and peasants, was the fact that they were knights – fighting men pledged to help the king.

The greatest castles were those built by the king himself to guard the coast against invasion, to control a town or to command a crossroads. These castles he placed in the care of his *constables*. These were men whose duty it was to look after the castle, organise its defence in time of war, and keep it ready for the king if he should choose to visit it. Such royal castles were built in the most modern fashion and were usually kept well repaired. When new methods of defence were invented, the royal castles would be altered to bring them up-to-date again. This naturally cost a great deal of money. In the Middle Ages some kings spent a tenth of their money on building and repairing castles. Nowadays the government doesn't spend nearly as much of its money on defence.

Some of the richer barons were almost as wealthy as the king himself. Because they were the king's trusted friends they were expected to use their homes in his service: so their homes were fortified

Bamburgh Castle, Northumberland: The defences of this royal castle have been altered many times to keep them up to date.

and thus became castles. Some of them were as strong and as up-to-date as the king's own castles. In times of peace the king might come to visit them. In time of war he might send his knights to shelter in a baron's castle and help protect the countryside round about.

Poorer barons and ordinary knights had to make do with simpler castles. They did not really expect the king to visit them or send his troops to shelter in their castles. But there were often local riots and rebellions, and it was a sensible precaution to fortify their homes against attack. The castles of these poorer barons and knights were smaller and simpler than the great castles of the king and his friends, and they were often not so modern or well-repaired. Sometimes they were just comfortable houses with battlements and one or two towers. The king would probably not have considered them proper castles at all. But the men who owned them were very proud of them. Just as being a knight set them apart from the merchants and peasants, even if they weren't as rich or important as the king, so owning a castle set them apart from their neighbours. It marked them out as people of importance in their village or town. They copied the castles of the richer barons as closely as they could afford to, adding walls which often weren't quite strong enough and towers which weren't quite high enough. Having a castle of any sort was better than not having one at all!

There are a great many of these smaller, simpler castles to be found. Many of them are still privately owned, though very rarely are the owners descended from the men who built them. The larger castles of the richer barons and the king are set further apart. You will need to travel greater distances to find them. Often they are empty ruins, looked after by the government so that people can visit them. There is usually a guide-book on sale inside which will tell you who built the castle and lived there. You can make your own guess, however, as to whether he was a humble knight, a wealthy baron or even the king himself. Just look at the size of the castle, the height of the walls and the number of towers.

Building a castle was not quick or cheap. It might take five or ten years to complete a really big castle. There were two reasons for this.

Stokesay Castle, Shropshire, is a fortified manor house rather than a true castle; but its owner was probably very proud of it.

One was that building could go on only during the summer months, so all building work took twice as long as it would today. The other reason was that the owner could hardly ever afford to pay the workmen for more than a few months at a time. He had to spread the cost of a castle over several years.

Castles cost a lot. In the twelfth century, a small castle might be built for about £1,000 – that would be nearly a million pounds at present day prices. A large castle, with high walls and many towers, would have cost ten times as much! Think about this when you look at a castle.

The difference between the various people who built castles can also be seen in the places they chose to build them. Very few castles were built in really inaccessible places. Almost all of them were built close to the places they were meant to protect. The royal castle at Dover looms over the port which, even in the Middle Ages, was the main entry from France into England. Caernarvon Castle controls the

Menai Straits between Wales and Anglesey, which at that time was the last stronghold of Welsh resistance to English rule. Edinburgh Castle dominates the town which clusters at the foot of its great rock. In each case the castle served as a base for the knights who patrolled the countryside and enforced the king's orders. Castles of this sort were built on the hill, rock or peninsula nearest to the port, town, ford or crossroads they were meant to protect or control. The important thing was to choose a place where steep slopes, cliffs or marshy ground provided natural barriers against attack.

Some castles were built to be centres of local government rather than military forts (though they could also serve as forts on occasion if need be). Because local people needed to enter these castles fairly often, the castles had to be built where the greatest number of people were – in the towns and cities. For the lords of these castles, cliffs and marshes were less important than easy day-to-day access by the townsfolk. If the town was built in a valley the castle had to be built there too. To make up for the lack of natural barriers, the walls of such town castles had to be higher and the gates stronger than usual.

Most castles, however, were built by barons and knights to be their homes. From these castles they controlled the farms and forests that belonged to them. As a result, their castles were built wherever it was most convenient to have them. Their castles were not built as part of any great overall plan by the king to protect the country or to suppress rebellion, though the king could always take possession of them in emergencies. Providing he got the king's permission, a knight or baron could build his castle anywhere he liked on his own land. If he was fond of hunting he might build it close to a forest where deer or wild boar could be found. Often, however, he would build it in the middle of a village on the site of an older un-fortified house that had belonged to his father. In this way he provided himself with a much grander home while still keeping his local connections.

Military fashion also dictated where a castle should be built. During the Middle Ages it became fashionable to build castles with water-filled moats around the foot of their walls. Since water cannot be made to flow uphill, the new castles had to be built where water could

Bodiam Castle, Sussex, was built partly as a home for its owner, Sir Edward Dallyngrigge, and partly against French pirates.

be collected by damming a river or stream to form a moat. So if you see a castle perched high up on top of a hill it is likely to be quite an early one, built there before anyone had thought of having a water-filled moat. On the other hand, if you see a castle built low down in a valley and set neatly within a square water-filled moat, it is likely to be a late one, built some time towards the end of the Middle Ages.

Trying to work out why a castle is built where it is, and not somewhere else, is the hardest part of the Castle Detective's job. This is because the countryside round the castle has often changed, even though the castle itself may look much the same as it has always done. New towns and villages have grown up around some castles which once stood in open country. In other places the town or village which stood at the gates of a castle has vanished. There may be only a few grassy mounds in a field to show you where it once stood. Lakes and marshes may have dried up, or new ones formed, since the castle was abandoned. The forests which sheltered the animals the castle

inhabitants were so fond of hunting will probably have been cut down.

Even so, the clues usually remain. A few enquiries will tell you whether the town surrounding your castle is an old one or a new one built since the castle fell into ruin. Banks and hollows in a nearby field, or even the name of the field itself, may indicate where a village or town once stood. Field names may also reveal whether there was a marsh or forest.

Remember that wherever castles were built, they were meant to look impressive. Even a small castle towered above the roofs of the peasants' houses. Painted white, the castle's walls and towers would have gleamed in the sun. Everyone could see the castle from a long way off and know that someone important lived there. The appearance of a castle often mattered as much as its strength. The lord of the castle wanted people to know when he was at home and would order his own special flag to be hoisted on a flagpole high on a tower. Even today you can tell whether the Queen is at home by looking to see whether her flag is flying from the flagpole on top of Buckingham Palace or Windsor Castle.

Check-list 1: Why is it there?

What was the castle built to do?

To guard a sea port?
To command a bridge or ford across a river?
To block a pass?
To control a town?

Why is the castle where it is?

Is it on a hill top, with steep slopes on all sides?
Is it on the edge of a cliff, so that strong defences were needed on only
   two or three sides?
Is it in a valley, where water could be found to fill a moat?
How far could you see from the castle? Could you see an enemy
   coming a long way off?
From how far away could people see the castle and know that its lord
   was keeping an eye on them?

Was the castle all alone?

Was there a village or town built close to the castle gates?
If there was, is it still inhabited or has it been deserted?

How long did it take to build the castle?

Is the castle just a motte and bailey castle that could be built in a year?
Is the castle a medium-sized one, with less than eight towers, that
   could be built in five years?
Is the castle a huge one that would take more than five years to build?
(Remember, the castle may have been built in several stages.
   Chapter 2 will help you discover whether it has.)

18   How much did the castle cost?

Is the castle a small one that would cost only £100,000 if it was built today?

Is the castle a medium-sized one that would cost about £1 million if it was built today?

Is the castle a huge one that would cost nearly £10 million if it was built today?

What sort of person built the castle?

The answers to the last two questions will give you an idea as to whether the lord was a rich knight, a baron or the king.

Look in the nearest church: some of the people who lived in the castle may be buried there.

Chapter 2
How old is it?

When William the Conqueror brought his Norman knights to England in September 1066 he knew he would have to fight hard to capture the country. His knights had an advantage over the Saxons who had not yet adopted the habit of fighting in armour on horseback. Even so, they needed safe places to dismount and rest – and they needed them quickly. There was no time to quarry stone, load it onto carts and transport it to where it was needed. There was no time to get lime for mortar. The first castles had to be built from what could be found close by – wood and earth!

Every Saxon knew how to dig, and every Saxon village had a carpenter. They could be made to construct a wall of earth and timber with a deep ditch in front of it very quickly, perhaps in two or three weeks. A really elaborate castle of earth and timber might take almost a year to complete, but it was still quicker than a stone castle.

For the first few years after the Norman Conquest most castles were made in this way, as the Norman armies fought their way westwards and northwards from Hastings. Garrisons of knights and archers were stationed in hastily-built forts to control roads, river-crossings and towns. As the years passed some of these early wooden forts were abandoned. Others, especially those built in towns, were kept and improved. One way of improving them was to build a great mound (called a *motte*) at one side of the courtyard (or *bailey*). From a wooden tower on this mound archers could pick off enemies in any direction.

When you find a castle with a large motte built at one side of the courtyard, you can be fairly sure that it was built by the Normans. In England very few mottes were built after AD 1150. If your castle is in England and it has a motte, it was almost certainly started before that date. That's your first clue – and it's a pretty big one! Even in a small castle the motte will still be 5 metres or more in height. Some mottes are more than 12 metres high. The biggest of all is at Thetford in Norfolk: it is 21 metres high!

The Normans didn't reach Scotland until about AD 1100 and it wasn't until AD 1170 that they crossed to Ireland. By that time mottes were rather out-of-date in England. But in Scotland and Ireland the Norman knights found conditions very like those their great-great-grandfathers had found in England in 1066. Once again they needed castles that could be built quickly from materials that could be found close at hand. In Scotland, therefore, a castle with a motte is likely to have been built between AD 1100 and AD 1200. In Ireland a castle with a motte is likely to have been built between AD 1170 and AD 1220.

Once built, mottes went on being used for a very long time. As late as AD 1348 the Earl of Stafford built himself a new house, with battlements and towers at the corners, on top of a motte built two hundred and seventy years earlier during the Norman Conquest. The Earl had made himself very rich and he wanted to impress everyone with his new house. So he put it high up on the old motte where everyone could see it!

'Motte and bailey' castles are found all over Britain. They were

Underneath the later walls and towers of Windsor Castle, Berkshire, you can still see the shape of the Norman motte and bailey castle.

the most common type of Norman castle, but today they are often unrecognised and misunderstood. This is not surprising. Wood rots if you bury its end in the ground and so the wooden walls and towers have collapsed and disappeared. If the castle was abandoned before stone walls were added it may even look like a part of the natural landscape. But the motte is easy to spot. Indeed, it's hard to miss it — even when it's overgrown with trees or bushes.

Beside the motte was the lower courtyard or *bailey*, originally protected by a ditch, a rampart and a wooden wall or *palisade*. Sometimes the defences of the bailey survive just as grassy banks or ridges in a field. Sometimes they have later stone walls and towers on them, as at Windsor. In towns, the bailey may have vanished completely under streets and houses. But the shape of the bailey can usually be traced by looking at the shape of the streets. Names like 'Castle Street' or 'Walls Lane' are useful clues.

Some castles had two baileys. The outer one was for farm buildings or store sheds. The inner one was for the more important buildings which could not fit on top of the motte: the lord's hall and kitchen, his chapel, the stables for his horses, workshops for the armourer, blacksmith and carpenter, barracks for the soldiers, and of course a well. The entrance to the bailey was protected by a big gate-tower with a portcullis and drawbridge. This was where visitors first entered the castle, and so the lord of the castle usually made the gate-tower as impressive as possible. Passing through the bailey, visitors would be led up a flight of steps to the top of the motte. Here the lord of the castle would meet them in his wooden tower, protected by another palisade.

None of these wooden buildings, towers or palisades survive now, though later stone ones may be there instead. By digging through the soil very carefully, archaeologists can discover exactly what these castles looked like. But you will have to use your own imagination to work out how they looked when the ramparts and the motte were of newly-dug earth, instead of being covered by grass, and when the palisades and towers were covered with clay and whitewashed to make them look as much like a stone castle as possible.

You will need to make your imagination work quite hard to do this. The grass-grown remains of a motte and bailey castle do not look very warlike; nor do they look much like someone's home! Yet in such castles the Norman knights and barons held their courts, feasted, and practised fighting. Here their wives lived, and here their children grew up playing games in the bailey amongst the soldiers and the horses.

Although these castles look as though they were quite simple, they were very effective in holding out against surprise attacks. They could also be made quite comfortable to live in. They had one very great drawback, however: they didn't last long! Even if they weren't burned down by the enemy, the timber walls and towers rotted so quickly that they needed to be replaced every thirty years or so. As a result, the Norman lords replaced the timber with stonework as soon as they could.

Stone walls take time to build and they cost money. Not every village had a mason, and not every mason knew how to build a castle. Usually a specialist mason had to be employed. A quarry would have

to be found and carts hired to carry the stone. Timber had to be felled to make scaffolding. Lime had to be brought in to make mortar. The lord of the castle would have to think very carefully before he decided to rebuild his castle in stone.

Some lords started work very soon after the Norman Conquest, when their motte and bailey castles were still quite new. Some of them were very wealthy. Others lived in places where danger threatened every day and a fire-proof stone castle was essential if they wanted to stay alive! Obviously, those lords who lived near stone quarries had an advantage. The cost of carting stone from the quarry to the castle would be less, and so the castle would be much cheaper to build.

Often, when you visit a castle you will find that the timber palisade around the top of the motte has been replaced by a stone wall. Originally this wall would have had battlements, but only in a few castles do these still remain. Such stone walls round the tops of mottes

The buildings inside shell keeps were usually of timber. Here at Restormel, Cornwall, they were of stone and so they have survived.

are called *shell keeps*. The great tower on top of the motte at Windsor is
a shell keep, though most people who go there do not realise this.
Inside their shell keeps the Norman lords built houses in a ring, with a
small courtyard in the middle. The backs of the houses leaned against
the stone wall. The houses were usually built of timber and clay, and
have long since rotted away. If you look carefully, however, you may
be able to see a line of square holes in the wall about 4 or 5 metres
above the ground. This is where the clay and timber houses were
joined to the stonework. The holes will be quite large – at least 30
centimetres square. (Don't confuse them with any smaller holes you
may find which are about 10 to 15 centimetres square. These were for
wooden scaffolding which was taken down as soon as the masons had
finished building the wall. Nearly every castle is covered with these
small scaffolding holes.) You may also find fireplaces built into the
stone wall, because it was safer to build them there than in the walls of
the timber houses.

Shell keeps stayed in fashion from about AD 1100 until about
AD 1180. A shell keep could not be built on a newly-made motte, since
its weight would have caused the motte to collapse. If you find one,
therefore, you will know that it must have been the son or grandson of
the first castle-builder who, sometime between AD 1100 and 1180,
decided to rebuild the old wooden castle he had inherited.

Just as the Norman lords replaced the palisade round the top of
the motte with a new stone wall, so they also rebuilt in stone the
palisade round the bailey courtyard. Sometimes they built the new
wall on top of the old rampart. Sometimes they cleared the rampart
away and started from scratch. The new walls were quite simple, but
they were very thick – usually 2 to 3 metres thick. This was so that they
could not easily be knocked down by a battering ram. On top of the
wall was a sentry-walk protected by a stone screen or *parapet*. To make
it easier for the soldiers to defend the castle the parapet had gaps in it,
called *crenels*, through which the soldiers could lean out to fire arrows
or throw spears at the enemy. The bits of parapet between the crenels
were called *merlons*. At first the crenels were quite far apart, with long
merlons between them. As time went by, however, it was found best to

have more crenels placed closer together. Today we call these lines of crenels and merlons *battlements*.

Faced with such stone walls, the enemy usually tried to get into the castle by attacking the gate into the bailey – so the wooden gate-tower also had to be rebuilt in stone. Sometimes, the gate-tower was the first part of the castle to be rebuilt in stone. Norman gate-towers were square or rectangular in plan, and two or three storeys high. You entered the castle through an arched passage in the lower part of the tower.

Because the gateways were so frequently attacked, castle-builders spent a lot of time thinking how to make them better. As a result, many Norman gate-towers were altered or completely rebuilt. Sometimes the shape of the windows was changed, or an outer gateway or *barbican* was added. But if you find a smallish square gatehouse with a round-topped entrance arch and the remains of round-topped windows, then you can be fairly sure it was built by the Normans some time between AD 1080 and 1180.

No matter how strong the bailey walls might be, or how well-defended the gateway, there was always the risk that the enemy would succeed in getting in. An inner stronghold was needed where the defenders could hope to hold out until help arrived. With the castles of the Norman Conquest, this inner stronghold was of course the motte with its timber palisade and tower. Where there was no motte, the Norman conquerors were able to try out a different solution to the problem of providing an inner stronghold. This was the *keep*.

The earliest Norman keeps were just big stone houses. To a Norman lord, a comfortable house was one with a large business room or *hall* where he could hold a court or meet his friends, a smaller private *chamber* where he could eat and sleep with his family, and a *chapel* where he could pray. To make such a house safe it needed to be built at first-floor level above a basement. In this position it would be out of reach of enemies with battering rams. The basement had no outside door and its windows were made too small for anyone to climb through. To get into the house you went up an outside stair of wood or stone to a door set high up in the side of the building. The walls of the house were made very thick indeed – sometimes as much as 4 metres.

When the lord did not intend to live in the castle all the time, he would build an extra set of rooms on top of the first set, rather like a block of flats. On the ground floor would be the basement, dark and used only for storage or for keeping prisoners. Above this, and entered by the stone or wooden outside stair, would be an apartment for the constable who looked after the castle when the lord wasn't there. Above this again, and reached only by an inside staircase hidden in the thickness of the wall, would be a second apartment for the use of the lord of the castle whenever he visited it. Each apartment had a hall, a chamber, and sometimes a chapel. The walls of these two apartments were well above the level of the ground outside and so were out of the reach of battering-rams. As a result, they could be hollowed out to make extra little rooms and passages.

The few keeps built by William the Conqueror and his friends were intended to look very grand. They were meant to impress the Saxons, most of whom would never have seen such massive buildings

The Tower of London: William the Conqueror's great keep, known as the White Tower.

before. The White Tower, which stands at the heart of the Tower of London, is 35 metres long, 32 metres wide and 27 metres high. It was the king's house, and as such it was the most important building in the castle. The entire castle has taken its name from it, for it is the true 'tower of London'. The hall and chamber of each apartment were built side by side, but the curved end of the chapel stuck out from the side of the big square building. The main entrance was by way of a wooden stair placed against the outside wall of the building.

The sons and grandsons of the men who came to England with

The Norman keep at Rochester, Kent. Notice the stone stairs leading up to the doorway. There was a chapel in the room above the entrance.

William the Conqueror in AD 1066 found these arrangements had some disadvantages. They built their stairs of stone and placed them inside a special building along one side of the keep. In the upper part of this extra stair-building they built their chapels.

Norman keeps of this later sort are easy to spot. Even when ruined they are usually the largest buildings in the castle. Square or rectangular in plan, with very thick walls, they often have small turrets at the corners. The main door is always about 5 metres above the ground and is reached by a stone stair which passes through a lower building built against the keep. Inside, each apartment is divided into a hall and chamber by a cross-wall; this sometimes has arches through it. The chapel is usually over the entrance stair. The thick walls are honeycombed with extra rooms and passages. Often the shape of the doors and windows will have been altered by later owners. If any of the original Norman ones still remain they will have round-topped arches.

Square Norman keeps like this were built mainly by the sons and grandsons of the men who fought at the battle of Hastings in AD 1066. So if you find one it will probably have been built some time between AD 1100 and 1180.

Hiding inside your keep until the enemy went away was one way of remaining safe. But while you were in the keep the enemy could burn down all the buildings in the bailey! Some way had to be found of keeping the enemy out of the bailey altogether. Not only had the gateway to be protected by a stone gate-tower, the walls themselves had to be made more difficult to attack. In particular, battering rams had to be kept away from the foot of the wall. The problem was that in order to fire an arrow or throw a spear at someone standing close to the foot of the wall, you had to lean far out over the battlements – and while you were leaning out you might be shot by an enemy archer!

The solution found by the castle-builders was to set square towers along the line of the bailey wall so that the towers projected in front of it. From the tops of the towers, and from arrow-slits in the sides, archers could shoot along the line of the wall. In this way they could keep the enemy away without being shot themselves. Each tower had

to be quite close to the next one, so that no part of the wall was out of range for the defending archers.

Some Norman lords experimented with these square *wall-towers* soon after the Norman Conquest. But the idea was slow to catch on, and it wasn't until a hundred years or more after the Conquest that wall-towers really became fashionable. They didn't remain in fashion for very long, however. So if you do find a square wall-tower, you can be fairly sure it was built some time between about AD 1160 and 1215.

Square wall-towers and square keeps went out of fashion because they suffered from the same disadvantage: their corners were easily attacked.

If you want to make a building collapse by tunnelling underneath it, or by hurling boulders at it with a giant catapult, the best place to start is at a corner. King John found this out in AD 1215 when he attacked the castle at Rochester in Kent, which was being held by rebels. He ordered his troops to dig a tunnel under one corner of the

The square wall-towers of Framlingham, Suffolk, show that the castle was built at the end of the 12th century.

great square keep. The roof of the tunnel was propped up with wooden logs. When the tunnel was finished it was filled with bundles of sticks. Then King John ordered his soldiers to set fire to the sticks. As they caught fire, they burned away the logs holding up the roof of the tunnel: and when the tunnel eventually collapsed, so did the corner of the keep above! King John's soldiers were then able to climb into the keep through the hole in the corner where the stonework had collapsed.

Once he had captured the castle King John had to set about repairing the keep. The damaged corner had to be rebuilt. To make sure no-one would be able to play the same trick on him, King John ordered that the new corner should be rounded. In this way, there would be no sharp angle for an enemy to tunnel under.

News of King John's successful attack on Rochester soon spread, and many people started experimenting with towers that were round in plan, rather than square. Round wall-towers in particular were found to be very useful. The wall-towers guarded the main wall

The round towers of Conway, Gwynedd, show that the castle was built in the 13th century.

around the castle, and this was where the enemy had to attack first. Boulders hurled by giant catapults bounced off the rounded walls of the new towers. After the attack on Rochester in AD 1215 most castle-builders used round towers.

This change of shape is a useful clue when you are trying to work out how old a castle is. If the wall-towers are square they will date from about AD 1160 to AD 1215. If they are rounded, they were built after AD 1215. If there is a mixture of both sorts, then you will know that someone has improved an old castle by adding towers in the new style after AD 1215.

Some lords tried using round keeps as well, and for a while these became very fashionable. No-one felt like pulling down a square keep just to rebuild it in a new shape – that would have been far too expensive! Those lords who already had square keeps went on living in them. However, where a new castle was being built, or a keep was being added to an old one, the new rounded shape was used. As it happened, England and Wales were then at war and so new building

A round keep. This one is at Launceston, Cornwall. It stands within an earlier Norman shell keep.

was needed along the Welsh borders. As a result, a lot of the castles there have round keeps, built during the period from AD 1215 to about AD 1250.

Round keeps did present some problems to those who built them and lived in them. True, they were much safer to live in: but it was not so easy to plan the sort of rooms and passages that could be built in the walls of a square keep. So while a few round keeps were built after AD 1250, they were exceptions. By that date, most lordly families in England had got castles — some with square keeps and some with round ones. Where new keeps were needed after AD 1250 they tended to be square or rectangular in plan. Set within new, safer bailey walls guarded by wall-towers, these later keeps were built for comfort rather than for strength.

The idea of a keep built for strength and security lingered on in Scotland and Ireland, however. Hitherto, castles in these countries had been built in much the same way as castles in England. The Norman lords who conquered Scotland and Ireland had kept in touch with their relations in England and Wales and followed the same fashions in castle-building. Gradually, however, the Irish and Scottish chieftains developed a new sort of castle which was much more suited to their needs. This was the *tower house*.

A tower house was a sort of keep. That is, the rooms were set one on top of another, instead of beside each other as in a modern house. But whereas a Norman keep formed an inner stronghold set within the castle walls, a tower house usually stood alone. Sometimes there was a small courtyard attached to one side of the tower house: in Scotland this was called a *barmkin* and in Ireland a *bawn*. These little courtyards were used to shelter animals, and did not have many buildings in them.

At first sight a tower house looks very like a Norman keep. It is square in plan, though it is usually not as big as a square keep. The door is at first-floor level, though unlike a square keep there is no stair-building protecting the door. The main difference is at roof level. Tower houses often have tall roofs showing above the battlements. The battlements themselves are set out in front of the walls, with a line of holes below them through which hot water and stones could be dropped on the heads of the enemy. These holes are called *machicoulations*, and they can be found on English and Welsh castles as well. But they *never* occur on square keeps. So if you see what looks like a small square keep with machicoulations round the top, you will know it is a tower house.

Inside, the arrangement of rooms is much the same as in a keep, but there are important differences. These are the clues. Firstly, each

Hermitage, Borders. The savage raids across the border between England and Scotland are reflected in the grim appearance of this tower house.

floor has just one big room; it is not divided into a hall and chamber, as in a keep. Secondly, the lowest room and the uppermost room each have arched stone ceilings, called *vaults*. These stone ceilings mean that the rooms in-between were fire-proof – a big improvement on the Norman square keep!

The lowest room was often used as a kitchen. On the floor above, where the main door is, was the hall. Above this was the chamber. Sometimes there was a second chamber on top, making four square rooms in all. Because there was no stair-building in which the chapel could be set over the stairs, as in a square keep, the chapel had to be very small indeed. Often it was just one corner of the chamber.

The Scottish and Irish chieftains started building these tower houses about AD 1350. This sort of castle stayed in fashion for some three hundred years – which shows how useful it was. A tower house wasn't as comfortable or as grand to look at as a Norman keep, but it was cheaper and quicker to build. Although it had thinner walls than a keep, and so could not withstand attack so well, it was just what was needed in those areas where a sudden raid was more to be feared than a long drawn-out siege.

In Scotland and Ireland you are more likely to find a tower house than any other form of castle. The idea was copied in northern England as well, where the same sort of raiding was common. However, the Scottish chiefs went on building tower houses long after the English and Welsh lords had given up living in castles altogether. These later Scottish tower houses often have very elaborate roofs indeed.

If, then, you find a square tower standing by itself, with a tall roof and with machicoulations below the battlements, you will know it is a tower house, built some time between AD 1350 and AD 1650. If the roof is very elaborate, with small rooms jutting out beyond the corners of the main part of the tower and lots of decorated gables, then you will know that it was built some time between AD 1550 and AD 1650.

Whereas the Scottish and Irish chieftains built tower houses, castle-builders in England and Wales concentrated on improving the outer defences of their castles. They were still worried about the

This tower house at Claypotts, Tayside, shows the elaborate roofs fashionable in 16th-century Scotland.

possibility of an enemy tunnelling under their walls and towers and causing them to collapse. Making the wall-towers round in plan helped, of course, but something was needed to keep tunnellers away altogether. In the end they decided that the best thing to do would be to drown them!

To do this they dug a ditch round the castle in such a way that it could be filled with water and so become a *moat*. It didn't really matter whether the moat was deep or shallow, nor whether it was wide or narrow. Whatever the size of the moat, if an enemy tried to tunnel under the castle walls the water from the moat would leak through the roof of the tunnel, eventually flooding it and drowning the miners. Of course, some castles had been built on hill-tops, and water could not be made to flow into the ditch to make a moat. Gradually, however, the usefulness of moats was realised and new castles were built in the bottoms of valleys where rivers could be diverted to fill the ditches and make moats.

Moats started to become fashionable about AD 1250. Although it had taken the castle-builders two hundred years to invent the moat, once they had invented it they never stopped using it. Moats remained in fashion until castles stopped being built altogether. If you find a castle without a moat, it may mean that the castle was built before AD 1250; but it may just mean that the castle was built too high up for a moat. Be careful! Try and think whether water could have been made to flow into the ditch. On the other hand, if you find a castle with a moat, it was probably built – or rebuilt – after AD 1250.

Using all these clues, you should be able to work out how old a castle is, just by looking at it, before you have even got inside! Some castles are very easy. If you find a square or rectangular castle, with round corner towers, set within a square or rectangular moat, then you will know it must have been built after AD 1250, since by that time both round towers and moats were in fashion. Most castles, however, were altered or enlarged from time to time as fashions changed. Some parts of the castle will be of one date, some parts will be of a different date. These castles are more difficult – but not too difficult for a Castle Detective! First you must look at the shape of the wall-towers; look for a keep showing above the battlements; see if there is (or was) a moat. Then look back at the clues given in this chapter. To make it easier, you may like to use the check lists on pages 41 and 42.

Check-list 2: How old is it?

What is the general shape of the castle?

If the shape is regular and compact, then the castle was probably built in the fourteenth or fifteenth century.

If the shape is sprawling and irregular, the castle is more likely to have been built in the eleventh, twelfth or thirteenth century.

(But the general shape is only a rough guide. You will need to look carefully at the different parts of the castle.)

Is there a motte?

If there is, the castle was started by the Normans sometime between AD 1066 and AD 1220, depending on which country you're in.

See page 20.

Is there a shell keep on the motte?

If there is, then it was built between AD 1100 and 1180. The motte must have been built much earlier.

Is there a square keep?

If there is, and it is in England, it was built between AD 1100 and 1180; in Scotland and Ireland square keeps can be later. (Remember, don't confuse a square keep with a tower house.)

Is there a round keep?

If there is, it was probably built between AD 1215 and 1250. Some clever castle-builders were trying out round keeps before AD 1215, but there weren't many of them.

What shape are the wall-towers?

If they are square, they were probably built between AD 1160 and
  1215. But square wall-towers came back into fashion in the fifteenth
  century, so be careful!
If they are round, they were built sometime between AD 1215 and
  about AD 1400.

What shape is the gatehouse?

If it is square, with round-arched windows, then it was built by the
  Normans between AD 1080 and 1180.
If it has a round tower at each side, it was built after AD 1215. This sort
  of gatehouse stayed in fashion a long time.

Is there a tower house?

If there is, it was built between AD 1350 and 1650.
If it has a very elaborate top, with small rooms jutting out beyond the
  main part of the tower, then it was built between AD 1550 and 1650.

Is there a moat?

If there is, it was probably dug after AD 1250. Remember that the
  castle may have been built long before then.

Chapter 3
How was it defended?

In the Middle Ages armies were usually much smaller than modern armies. The king or baron would call the knights to whom he had given land to come to his aid fully armed. These knights would bring any other knights to whom they had passed on some of the land. The king or baron might also hire extra foot-soldiers and archers, or knights who hadn't been given any land and who made a living fighting for whoever would pay them. With this army the king or baron could defend his own castles or attack the castles of other people.

A castle was meant to protect the people inside it from attack. The men who designed and built castles had to imagine in what way their castles might be attacked, and then think of a way of preventing the attack from being successful. If you want to be able to understand how castles were defended, you must first think about how they were attacked!

Not every castle was fully manned all the time. No-one, not even the king, could afford to pay for all the knights and archers necessary to defend a castle for more than a month or two. For much of the time, castles were occupied by the constable and his family and just a few soldiers. So there was always a chance of capturing a castle by taking its defenders by surprise, before the constable had time to summon extra knights and archers. Anyone who wanted to attack a castle always tried to take it by surprise. Sometimes the attackers even tried to climb up the drains which emptied the toilets and get into the castle that way. Rather a dirty trick, this!

If the surprise attack didn't succeed, the castle would have to be taken by assault. This meant building ladders, setting them against the walls and trying to climb over the walls before the defenders could stop you. It is difficult to climb a ladder in full armour, carrying a sword or spear — especially if someone is firing arrows at you, or hurling down large boulders on your head. The defenders might even use long poles to push the top of the ladder away from the wall and make it topple over, killing or injuring all those who were on the ladder at the time.

Almost as dangerous was the attempt to get close enough to the bailey gatehouse to be able to set fire to the wooden gates or to knock them down with a log used as a battering-ram. Sometimes the attackers put their battering-ram under a wooden shed, called a *cat* or *sow*, to protect the men using the battering-ram from stones and arrows. Even so, attacking the gates in this way was still a dangerous business, especially if the defenders used fire-arrows to set fire to the cat.

If these methods didn't work, the attackers had to find a way of knocking down a section of the defences. This meant battering the

walls with huge boulders until the walls crumbled. The earliest machine used for this purpose was the catapult or *mangonel*. This had a long arm with a spoon-shaped end, mounted on a wooden frame. Rope was wound round and round the end of the long arm and fixed to the frame. A boulder was placed in the spoon-shaped part, and the rope was twisted tightly with levers. When the long arm was released, the rope started to untwist very quickly, jerking the long arm upright and hurling the boulder into the air. A mangonel could throw a boulder the size of a football over 100 metres. You could try making a small one, using matchboxes, elastic and small pieces of wood.

In the Middle Ages elastic hadn't been invented. The twisted ropes of the mangonel were affected by damp, so that the machine sometimes threw its boulders too far or not far enough. This meant that it was difficult to keep pounding the same bit of wall until it fell down. A new machine was needed which was more accurate.

This new machine was the *trebuchet*. It was a sort of catapult, but instead of using twisted ropes it worked like a huge see-saw. One side of the see-saw was very long and had a rope sling on the end. The other end was very short and had a large box on the end into which weights could be put. You worked the machine by hauling down the long end so that the empty box on the other end rose up into the air. Then you put your boulder in the sling and tied the sling down while you put lots of other boulders into the box. When you untied the sling the heavy box dropped downwards making the other end of the see-saw rise into the air, hurling the boulder out of the sling towards the target. Because the machine worked by gravity, and because gravity doesn't change, the machine always worked the same way whatever the weather! You could try making a model of a trebuchet and compare it with your model mangonel.

A big trebuchet could hurl quite heavy weights a very long way.
It could hurl a stone weighing 150 kilogrammes more than 100 metres.
Sometimes, however, trebuchets were used to hurl nastier things. One
old picture shows a trebuchet loaded with a dead horse. It had
probably been dead a long time and so was rotten and full of germs.
When it was hurled over the castle wall and landed in the bailey it
would break apart and splatter everyone with rotten flesh and germs.
In this way the attackers tried to introduce disease into the castle in
the hope that the defenders would fall sick and have to surrender.
Nowadays we would condemn this sort of thing as 'germ warfare'.

Throwing rotten meat and germs around was always a rather
risky affair, however. After all, the attackers might catch the disease
too. A much more certain – though long drawn-out – method of
getting into a castle was by tunnelling. You will remember how King
John succeeded in capturing the keep at Rochester by getting his
soldiers to tunnel under one corner so that it collapsed. Tunnelling
was the method of attack the defenders feared most. They would know
it was going on because they would be able to see the loose earth being
carried away from the tunnel entrance. But they wouldn't be able to
do anything very much to stop it because they wouldn't know which
way the tunnel was being dug. Out of sight below ground, the miners
would be working their way towards the castle and eventually – quite
suddenly – part of it would collapse with a crash and the enemy would
rush in through the hole in the wall.

If all these methods of attack failed, the attackers would have to
try to starve the defenders into surrender. Shut up in their castle and
unable to get fresh food, the defenders would have to ration their
supplies more and more strictly until all the food was gone. This might
take more than a month, but once all the food had been eaten the
defenders would have to surrender.

Everyone knew that a castle would eventually have to surrender.
No castle could hold out for ever, no matter how bravely it was
defended. The advantages weren't always on the side of the attackers,
however. Sieges were expensive and dangerous too. It cost a lot of
money to hire and feed enough knights, archers, foot-soldiers and

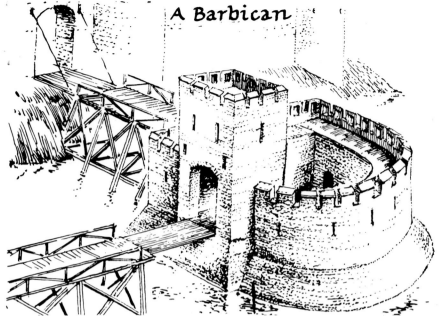

miners to attack a well-built castle. If the siege dragged on for week after week there was the danger that the attackers' own castles might be besieged while they weren't looking. During a siege there were always discussions going on between the leader of the attackers and the lord or constable of the castle. Sooner or later they would agree terms, and then the castle would be surrendered. Very few sieges were fought out to the bitter end.

A castle, then, was a means of keeping your enemy at bay while you discussed terms. The longer you kept the enemy out the better terms you could obtain. So how was a castle defended?

First of all, remember that if the attack came as a surprise there might not be many defenders in the castle – perhaps just ten or twenty people in all. Even when there was time for preparation, the defenders often did not number more than fifty. Archers and men-at-arms would need to rush from one part of the castle to another to beat off each attack. They would need to fire first from one arrow-slit and then from another, so as to make it seem that the castle was better defended than it really was.

Since the gateway was the weakest part of the castle, it had to be specially protected. Many castles had an outer defence or *barbican* to protect the bridge over the ditch or moat. This made it difficult for the enemy to get up close to the gates until he had first captured the barbican. Some barbicans were just long narrow passages, lined with a wall on each side, leading to the gatehouse. This sort of barbican herded the attackers into a small area in front of the gatehouse where it would be easier to kill them. Nowadays, most visitors rush through the gatehouse into the castle without thinking about what it was like in the Middle Ages: but the Castle Detective stops and looks for a barbican!

No matter how strong the wooden gates of a castle might be, they could eventually be broken down with a battering-ram. To use a battering-ram you needed to get up close to the gates. The best way to stop an enemy breaking down your gates was to remove part of the bridge over the moat or ditch. This part was the *drawbridge*.

The first drawbridges were very simple. The castle defenders just took away the planks of the bridge and carried them into the gatehouse! Soon, however, a better way was found. The part of the bridge nearest the gatehouse was made like a huge see-saw, balancing on the doorstep of the gatehouse. Half of the drawbridge projected forward over the ditch or moat, the other half projected backwards inside the gatehouse. In order to work like a see-saw, the inner end of the drawbridge had to swing down so that the outer end could swing up. A large stone-lined pit was therefore dug in the floor of the gatehouse just inside the entrance, so that the weighted inner end of the drawbridge could drop down into it. Drawbridges of this sort were called *turning-bridges*.

In some castles you will find that the drawbridge pit has been filled up, now that the drawbridge isn't used, but in many castles the pit is still open. If you look carefully at the sides of the pit, you may be

able to see the stone sockets where the metal axle of the bridge was set.

In the later part of the Middle Ages many castle-owners found this large pit in the floor of the gatehouse rather inconvenient. So another type of drawbridge was invented, called a *bascule bridge*. This was shorter than the turning-bridge. It was hinged on the outer edge of the doorstep of the gatehouse and was lifted by two large wooden beams, like cranes. These beams still worked like see-saws. They projected inside the gatehouse and had large weights on the inner ends. They didn't need large pits to drop into, but they did need slots in the outer wall of the gatehouse where the beams could lie when the bridge was up. When you see such slots you will know that the gatehouse had a bascule bridge. Bridges of this sort can still be found over modern canals in some places.

In the Middle Ages it was difficult to make locks strong enough to hold a door shut against a battering-ram. A much better arrangement was a large wooden beam placed across the back of the door. If you look in the side walls of the gate-arch, you will usually find a deep square hole about a metre or so above the floor, into which the beam could be slid when the door was opened.

Another sort of door was the *portcullis*. This slid up and down instead of being opened and shut, and took the form of a wooden grille fastened with iron. To hold it in place, the outer edges were set into grooves carved in the side walls of the gatehouse. When the drawbridge was down and the doors were open, the portcullis was hauled up into the room over the gateway by means of a wooden windlass. If danger suddenly threatened, the brake on the windlass

would be released and the great weight of the portcullis would send it crashing down to block the gateway below. This was the great advantage of the portcullis – once the man at the windlass decided to let it down, no-one could stop it. To make sure no-one even tried to stop it, the portcullis often had spikes on the bottom!

Some castles still have a portcullis. A few even have a windlass to pull it up. But even when the castle is a ruin, you can still work out whether there was once a portcullis by looking for two vertical grooves cut in the side walls of the gatehouse. They are usually about 15 centimetres wide and are cut about 10 centimetres deep in the stonework. Look carefully – there may have been more than one portcullis. Some gatehouses had as many as three!

Once an enemy had crossed the ditch, broken through the portcullis and hacked and battered his way through the great doors or gates, he found himself in a long passageway. At the other end of this passage there were usually more doors and often another portcullis. Having fought his way in, the enemy now had to fight his way out again into the castle bailey. This was a dangerous moment! Caught in this 'killing ground', no reinforcements could reach him. The way forward was blocked by the doors and portcullis, the way back was blocked by his own men. Hampered by his armour and weapons, and by the sheer numbers of his troops, he couldn't easily twist or turn to avoid missiles thrown by the defenders.

If you look at the side walls of the gatehouse, in the middle part of the passageway between the two sets of doors, you will often find arrow-slits. These were placed so that defenders standing in small rooms on either side of the passageway could shoot arrows into the mass of enemy troops trying to break down the doors. Look up! If the roof of the passageway is still intact you will probably see holes in it. Some people call these 'murder holes'. Through them the defenders could shoot arrows or poke spears at the enemy below. Some people believe that the defenders also used to pour boiling oil or melted lead through the holes.

Oil and lead were very expensive, however, and few castle-owners could have afforded to use them in this way. Also, there would have been the danger that the hot lead would set fire to the doors or portcullis, letting the enemy through into the bailey. It was important that the doors should not be burned down. If any liquid was poured through these 'murder holes' it is likely to have been cold water, to put out any fires lit against the doors by the enemy. These 'murder holes' were probably fire-extinguishers!

In the Middle Ages armies spent a great deal of time attacking the gatehouses of castles. It is worth taking time to look at them carefully. It may take you two minutes to walk through the passageway. It might have taken an attacker two weeks!

As you cross the bridge to the gatehouse, look first to see whether it has towers at the sides from which defenders could fire at an enemy

as he crossed the bridge. How many arrow-slits can you see? Look to see if there are slots in the wall over the entrance where the beams of a bascule bridge lay when the bridge was up. If there aren't any slots, then the drawbridge was probably a turning-bridge. Look for the drawbridge pit just inside the entrance.

Once inside the passageway, look for the grooves for a portcullis and for the draw-bar holes – the deep holes in the walls where the bars which locked the doors were kept. Doors need *jambs* to close against. Look for the vertical stone side-posts built into the walls. Count how many doors and portcullises there were. Was there a 'killing-ground' in the middle of the passageway between the doors? Go upstairs if you can, and look to see where the portcullis was hauled up through a slot in the floor into the room over the passageway.

With gatehouses so well-defended it was sometimes easier for the enemy to assault the walls of the castle. How were these defended? The walls had to be very thick: thick enough to resist battering-rams and to allow sentries to walk along the top. Look at the notches in the parapet, the *crenels*, cut to allow the defenders to lean out. Sometimes you can see grooves in the stonework at each side of the crenel, or iron hooks. These were for wooden shutters which closed the crenels when they weren't being used.

For complete safety it was better for the defending archers to shelter in the projecting wall-towers. From arrow-slits in the sides of these towers they could fire along the face of the wall. The arrow-slits or *loops* are very narrow on the outside: usually about 1 metre long, but only 10 centimetres wide. Inside the tower the sides of the loop splay out to make an opening between 1 metre and 2 metres wide. This opening is called an *embrasure*. The top of the embrasure may be flat, arched or pointed. Some embrasures are so large that they can contain two loops.

Using an arrow loop was not easy. Imagine standing in the embrasure and trying to fire a bow and arrow, or a cross-bow. Often the embrasure was not tall enough for a long-bow to be used, or wide enough for a cross-bow. Recently, some archaeologists and historians have experimented, using modern bows and arrows and medieval loops. They found that if you fire an arrow from a long-bow, it wobbles about for the first metre or so before the feathers on the end steady it. If you want to be sure of getting it through the 10 centimetres wide opening of the loop, you must stand well back – not in the embrasure at all, but on the floor of the tower about a metre away from the embrasure.

This makes sense. A good enemy archer could shoot in through the loop if he could get close enough. An embrasure was not a safe place to stand. The defenders probably worked in pairs: two archers together, or an archer and a 'spotter'. Standing at each side of the embrasure, the archer and his spotter could see quite a lot through the narrow opening of the loop. Once an enemy had been spotted, the archer would step quickly out in front of the embrasure and shoot his arrow. Then he would step back again to one side before anyone could shoot in through the loop and hit him. Try to imagine what it was like being a defending archer. How much of the outside world can you see through the loop? Are there any 'blind spots' where an enemy could hide without being seen?

This problem of blind spots worried the castle-builders. If you look at a castle's walls and towers you will sometimes see, just below the battlements, a row of holes about 20 to 30 centimetres square. When the castle was about to be attacked the defenders erected temporary wooden shelters called *hourds*. These were set on wooden beams pushed through those holes below the battlements, so that the hourds overhung the walls. Look carefully at these holes when you find them. Don't muddle them up with scaffolding holes, which will

cover the whole wall in a regular pattern, or with drain-holes which will slope downwards to allow rain water to run away.

Hourds were used a lot during the Middle Ages, and most castles show hourd-holes somewhere – on the walls, on the towers, on the gatehouse or even on the keep. The hourds allowed the defenders to climb out through the crenels so that they were directly above the enemy. Through holes in the wooden floor they could then pour liquids, drop heavy stones or shoot arrows at anyone below. The roofs over these wooden shelters protected the defenders from enemy arrows fired high into the air over the sides of the hourd.

A castle which was expecting an attack, and which had put up its hourds, would look very different from the way it looked in peace-time. The whole skyline of the castle would have been changed, making the castle look much more aggressive and threatening. When you look at a castle, try to imagine what it would have looked like with the hourds up, showing that the whole castle was in a state of defence.

Hourds were an important part of a castle's defences – but they had disadvantages. For one thing, they were made of wood. They were easy to set on fire or to break with the boulders thrown by mangonels or trebuchets. Also, it took time to get the pieces out of the castle store-room, carry them up to the battlements and assemble them. By the later part of the Middle Ages most castle-builders had decided to use the permanent stone hourds called *machicoulations*. These provided the same sort of 'balcony' effect, and had the same holes in the floor through which things could be poured or dropped on the enemy below. But they didn't have roofs, and they were built as part of the wall or tower.

By the end of the Middle Ages, when many of the old castle-owning families had died out and newly-rich knights were trying to show how important they now were, machicoulations became very elaborate indeed. Some castle-owners were more concerned about how their machicoulations looked than they were about how they worked. If you look closely, you will see that some of the grandest-looking machicoulations don't have any holes in the floor to drop things through. They are fakes, designed partly to frighten enemies away, but mainly to make the castle look grand!

Battlements, hourds, machicoulations and loops are all very well, but you must be able to reach them. When you visit a castle, think how

64   long it would take you to climb up to the battlements. Remember, you would be in armour and carrying a bow and arrows, or a sword and shield. Once you were on the battlements, how quickly could you get round to the other side of the castle if there was a sudden surprise attack there? And if your part of the battlements was over-run by the enemy, how easy would it be for you to escape into a nearby tower?

      If your castle was really well-defended, the enemy would just have to sit down outside and wait for you to starve. This is what the word 'siege' means – sitting down and waiting. Then you would need to ration your supplies, count the number of sides of beef, lamb or pork, count the barrels of salted fish or cheese. A sack of flour might be as important as a bundle of arrows. If you could hold out long enough your friends might come to your help, driving the enemy away. Or the enemy might get tired of waiting. Food and water were weapons too!

Check-list 3: How was it defended?

Is there any high ground close to the castle?

If there is, the enemy could put mangonels and trebuchets there to
  bombard the castle more easily.

Is there a moat?

If there is, how easy would it have been for the enemy to divert the
  stream which fills it? How easy would it be for him to drain the
  moat?

Can you see more than one ring of walls?

If you can, then the enemy would have to capture two castles, one set
  inside the other.

How many wall-towers are there?

Are the towers the right shape to stand up to mangonels and
  trebuchets?
Are the towers close enough together?
Can you see any blind-spots where an enemy could reach the castle
  wall without being seen from a tower?

How many arrow-loops and crenels can you see?

Are there enough loops and crenels all round the castle, or can you find
  a safe place to attack?
How long would it take you to run up to the walls? Remember, an
  archer can fire five or six arrows per minute! Would you make it?

Can you see any holes for wooden hourds?

If you can, were there hourds all along the walls, or only in certain
  places?

66   Can you see any machicoulations?

If you can, why do you think the castle-builder put them there and not somewhere else?

Is there a barbican?

If there is, does it form just an extra layer of defence? Or does it provide a 'killing ground' in front of the gatehouse?

How strong is the gatehouse?

Was there a drawbridge? How would you get across the ditch if the bridge was up?
Is there a machicoulation above the entrance?
How many portcullises were there?
How many pairs of doors were there?
Are there 'murder holes' in the ceiling of the passage?
Is there a 'killing ground' in the passage, with arrow loops on either side?

How easy was it to reach the battlements?

How did you get to the top of each tower, if you were a defender?
How did you reach the sentry-walk between the wall-towers?
How long would it take you to get from one side of the castle to the other?

Is there a keep (or shell keep)?

If the enemy captured the bailey, and you had to retire to the keep, how long could you hold out there while you discussed the terms of surrender?

Chapter 4
How did they live in it?

Food and drink didn't have to be weapons all the time. Usually they were just part of the day-to-day business of living. Banquets and feasts were important occasions in castle life. But every day was not a feast day, and banquets happened only every now and then. What was it like to live in a castle?

Every lord who decided to build a castle hoped that it would never be attacked. Indeed, its appearance was intended to frighten off enemies. Above all else, a castle was intended to be a home. It was the home not just of the owner: it was also the home of his servants and his soldiers. It had to have enough room for himself and his family, his guests, his servants, his knights and archers, his horses and all his stores. It had to have kitchens and toilets. It had to be comfortable – and it had to look comfortable. The inside of the castle had to impress visitors with its comfort as much as the outside impressed them with its military strength.

Think of all the people who had to live in a castle. There was the lord himself, of course, with his wife and his children. He might have quite a lot of children! He would have at least one man-servant, and his wife would have several maid-servants. There would be a cook and some kitchen servants to help prepare the food. There would be a priest to say Mass in the chapel. The priest would probably also act as the lord's secretary, because he was often the only person in the castle who could read and write. The lord's steward would be in charge of all these people.

As well as this group of people who surrounded the lord and his family, there were others who worked in the castle. There would be a carpenter, for instance, and an armourer who looked after the weapons. In a small castle he might also shoe the horses. There would be grooms for the horses, and huntsmen who looked after the hounds and the hawks. Then there would be the knights, archers and men-at-arms who formed the garrison.

If the lord was very rich and important, there would be many other people living in the castle. The castle was the centre of the lord's estate. He depended upon the food and the rent from the farms on his estate to keep his family. Running a great estate involved a lot of people, and some of these would live in the castle so as to be near their lord. A really rich baron might have more than a hundred servants of one sort or another! Many of these might be married, with families of their own, all living in the castle.

A castle was thus like a village, full of all sorts of people. Some old, some young; some well-dressed, some in rags. A large castle was more like a small town, with a constant coming and going of people, horses, carts and carriages. Every now and then the lord would decide to leave to stay in another of his castles or to visit a friend. He would take his family, his personal servants, his priest, his cook, his grooms and his

huntsmen — a great cavalcade of people on horseback, with carts carrying the mattresses for the beds, spare clothes, dishes and pans for the kitchen, and perhaps even a portable altar and stained glass for the chapel window.

When he arrived, there would be a great to-do! Rooms had to be found for all these people, stables for all the horses. Castles needed to be rather like hotels, ready to take in a sudden rush of guests. Worst of all was when the lord sent warning that he would be arriving with a number of guests, each of whom would be bringing his own family and servants! Then the steward would worry which rooms to allocate to which guests. Would some of them mind sharing rooms? Would some of them mind sharing beds? Would there be enough food? Would there be enough firewood? If not, someone would have to be sent out to buy more of whatever was needed.

At the beginning of the Middle Ages castles looked rather like small fortified towns. Inside the walls of the castle there were separate 'houses' scattered about the bailey. By the end of the Middle Ages, castles were built in neater shapes with the houses joined up to form ranges of buildings set round a courtyard. But even then they were still called 'the houses in the castle'.

Because they were set within the safety of the castle walls, the houses in the castle did not need to be built so strongly as the wall-towers or gatehouse. As a result, they have usually not survived the centuries of wind and rain so well. Often, when you visit a castle, you will find that while the outside seems almost complete, the inside is empty. The 'houses in the castle' have vanished.

To the Castle Detective this is a challenge. Are there clues as to what the houses in the castle looked like? What was this room used for? Why is there a fireplace half-way up that wall? Where did that stair lead to? Where was the kitchen? How far did you have to walk to the toilet? There are almost always clues to help you answer these questions, even when the houses in the castle seem completely ruined. Once again, it is a matter of using your eyes to spot the clues and working out what they mean.

Being the lord of a castle meant that you had certain public duties to perform on behalf of the king. To carry out these duties a lord needed a *Great Hall*. This was normally the largest room in the castle. It symbolised the lord's duties on behalf of the king, and so it was usually placed in an important position, where visitors could see it as soon as they entered the castle. So when you go through the castle gatehouse into the bailey, look for the remains of a large building standing where everyone could see it. The actual size will differ from castle to castle, but a Great Hall will usually be at least 12 metres long and 6 metres wide. In a really big castle it may be 25 metres long and 10 metres wide! If there is a keep, the Great Hall may be inside. But even when there is a keep, you will sometimes find that a new Great Hall has been built nearby at a later date.

Where the Great Hall was more than 7 metres wide, it would have been necessary to support the roof with one or two rows of pillars. They would have looked rather like the pillars in a church which divide the nave from the aisles. You may be able to find the remains of such pillars. Only at the end of the Middle Ages did carpenters manage to make roofs for buildings more than 7 metres wide without using pillars.

The Great Hall would have been as tall, or taller, than it was wide. From the floor you could look up and see the underside of the roof. Along the side facing the courtyard there would have been large windows, sometimes with stone seats built into them where people could sit and enjoy the sunlight. These windows would have been the largest in the castle. At the beginning of the Middle Ages, in the eleventh and twelfth centuries, the fire was usually in the middle of the

hall. The smoke escaped through a hole in the roof. But by the end of the Middle Ages most halls had a large fireplace built into a wall at the side of the hall. Sometimes the hearth itself, or the back of the fireplace, was made of red tiles set on edge. Look out for these – they are a useful clue. Above the fireplace was a chimney. To make sure the smoke went up the chimney there was usually a hood of stone or plaster jutting out above the fireplace. These hoods rarely survive now. If you look at each side of the fireplace you may be able to see the marks on the stone where the hood has broken off.

The Great Hall was used only occasionally. Most of the time it stood cold and empty. But on those occasions when it was used for a banquet, or to hold a court, there had to be somewhere to prepare the food. At one end of the Great Hall you will therefore usually find two smaller rooms with doors connecting them to the hall. These were the *buttery* (where wine and beer were served) and the *pantry* (where food was served). Beyond these two rooms there was the *kitchen*.

The kitchen is usually quite easy to spot. It had to have huge fireplaces where oxen, sheep or pigs could be roasted on spits. There may be as many as three or four fireplaces in the kitchen of a big castle. Look out for those red tiles set on edge. Near the kitchen would be a well for water. Try to imagine what it would have been like to work in a kitchen like this. Which was the quickest way to the well to fetch water when the cook was in a bad temper? Which way would you carry the hot food through to the pantry, where the hall servants would carve it, place it on dishes and carry it through into the hall? Even when these 'service rooms' are completely ruined, you should still be able to work out the answers to these questions if you look carefully at the ruined walls to see where the doorways were.

This arrangement of special rooms – Great Hall, pantry, buttery and kitchen – served the 'public' part of the lord's life. Usually these rooms were too big and too expensive to heat to be convenient for his private life. For this he needed a smaller and more comfortable house nearby.

Yet even when he was being private, the lord still needed a large formal room where he could entertain friends or carry out any business which didn't require the Great Hall. So he had a smaller *hall* of his own. This would have been easier to heat, but it still needed a large fireplace and windows with window seats, just like the Great Hall. Next to this hall would be his *chamber*, a room where he could retire with his family when he wanted peace and quiet. If he was rich enough to have a large castle, he might have several chambers — perhaps one for himself and his wife, one for his daughters and one for his sons. Often the rooms in the wall-tower nearest to the lord's hall were used as chambers in this way.

Remember that the houses in the castle often had two floors or storeys. If you look at the walls of the castle, about 3 or 4 metres above the ground, you will often see a row of empty holes in the stonework, each one about 30 centimetres square. These once held the wooden beams which supported a planked floor. The wooden floor has long since rotted away, leaving fireplaces, window seats and doorways

apparently suspended half-way up the wall. Next time you see a fireplace half way up a wall, look for the holes for the floor beams just below it. Try to imagine a room full of people up there!

When he was at home in his castle, the lord was expected to go to the *chapel* each day to hear Mass, together with his family. The chapel was usually built close to his house, so that he could reach it without getting wet if it was raining. If the lord's chamber was up on the first floor there was often a balcony in the upper part of the chapel where the lord could sit with his family. Everyone else stood below on the floor of the chapel. If you look up, you may be able to see the empty holes for the wooden balcony and the door leading from the lord's chamber.

How do you recognise a chapel? Well, it will have a separate entrance from the bailey, so that all the castle's inhabitants could use it. It will usually have an extra-large or extra-decorated window at the end furthest from the door. It won't have a fireplace. It may still have an altar, if you're lucky! However, the two easiest clues are these. Look for a small stone basin carved into the wall. This was called a *piscina*, and it was where the priest rinsed the sacred vessels used in the Mass. Look also for a stone seat with an arch over it, carved into the wall opposite the piscina. This was the *sedilia*, and it was a seat for the priest. With these two clues you can't go wrong. Only chapels have a piscina and a sedilia.

Remember that there may be more than one chapel in a castle. If he was very rich the lord of the castle might have a small private chapel quite separate from the larger chapel which served all the castle's inhabitants. Since there is often a chapel in the stair-building of a keep, above the entrance stair, look out for one there.

When more than one lordly family lived in a castle, each would expect an apartment of its own – a group of rooms comprising a hall and one or more chambers. If the lord's grown-up sons or his widowed mother lived in the castle, they would each expect an apartment of this sort. There had to be an apartment for the constable and his family if the lord intended to spend much time away from the castle. There had to be apartments for guests, too. In the Middle Ages, lords and ladies

quarrelled a lot about who was the most important, so it was best to give each visiting family a separate apartment if it could be arranged.

Identifying these various apartments is sometimes quite difficult. If the castle was built or re-built in the later part of the Middle Ages (in the fourteenth or fifteenth centuries), all the accommodation may have been joined up to form a great labyrinth of rooms on two or even three floors. When the castle is badly ruined, even the best Castle Detective has trouble working out which room was which! You will have to set your imagination working extra hard, guided by the clues which can be found.

First of all, although it may look as if all the rooms connect with each other, especially if only the lower parts of the walls survive now, this is rarely the case. The rooms fall into groups. Look at the walls. Are those gaps really doorways, or are they just where the wall has been broken away? A proper doorway will have *jambs* carved in the stonework at the sides, against which the door would have shut. (Look at the doors in your own house and see how they close against jambs carved into the wooden door-frame.) Think about the rooms upstairs in the castle. How could you get there? Where is the nearest stair? If you couldn't get there without going outside into the rain, then the rooms upstairs probably aren't part of the same apartment as the rooms downstairs. Would you want to go out of your front door to reach the stair every time you had to go to bed?

The door opening from the bailey courtyard into a 'house' often had a bolt in the form of a large bar of wood sliding across the back of the door. Look for the square hole in the doorway into which the bolt slid when it wasn't being used. It will be like the bolt holes you found in the gate-house as you came in, but a bit smaller. In the Middle Ages people liked to be private whenever they could. How private do you think these rooms were? To reach one room, did you have to go through another? If so, the rooms were probably part of the same apartment.

A very important person would expect to have somewhere completely private. He wouldn't want a room through which other people walked to reach their rooms. So look at the door jambs again. Which way did the doors open? If you look at your own bedroom you will find that the door opens inwards into the room, not outwards onto the landing or passage. Private rooms always have doors that open inwards. So if you are looking for an apartment for an important person, look for a series of rooms with their own front door opening inwards from the courtyard. The rooms will interconnect, so that the different members of the occupant's family could pass from one part of the apartment to another. They will form a group quite separate from any other group of rooms in the castle.

Now look at how comfortable these rooms were. The more

79

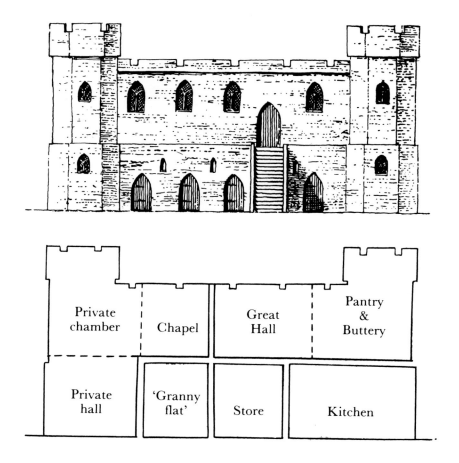

This house has five front doors! If you look carefully, you will see that the Great Hall, pantry and buttery are up on the first floor. The lord of the castle has a 3-room private apartment at the other end of the house. The kitchen and store on the ground floor serve both these apartments, and also the separate 'granny flat' for the lord's mother.

comfortable the rooms, the more important the person who lived there. Were the rooms well lit by large windows? Rooms for important people were often built at first floor level. Up there it was safe to have large windows, because they were out of reach of attackers or burglars. Were the rooms warm in winter? Look for fireplaces. A chamber, whether it was for a guest or for a resident of the castle such as the steward or butler, had to have a fireplace.

How convenient were the rooms? A really important guest would expect to be lodged somewhere near the lord of the castle, not stuck away in some corner at the far end of the courtyard. How many rooms had their own toilets? Important people didn't want to have to share a toilet with strangers!

Toilets are usually quite easy to find. Look for a small room about 1 metre square, opening off a larger room or reached by a narrow passage. Often such toilets, called *garderobes*, were hollowed out in the thickness of the walls. They are small and dark with low ceilings. Sometimes you will find the stone toilet-seat still in position. Below the seat you will find a rectangular shaft running down through the thickness of the wall. Many of these shafts merely emptied through a hole in the castle wall into the ditch or moat. These toilets could not be flushed like a modern toilet, so they must have been very smelly. They must also have been cold, draughty and rather unpleasant to use. They were called 'garderobes' because people often kept their robes and clothes there. They believed that the smell would keep the moths away! This is the origin of our word 'wardrobe'.

When the garderobe shaft emptied into a special room or box, this would have to be emptied from time to time. A low arch was usually built connecting it with the outer face of the castle wall. Some unfortunate boy would occasionally be pushed through this arch and told to rake out the contents into the castle ditch. There can't have been many volunteers for this job!

Toilets like this were always a weakness in the castle's defences. However narrow you made the shafts, there was always the danger that an enemy might persuade some very thin soldier to wriggle up the shaft into the castle and then open the gates to his friends. Some very famous castles were captured in this way, including one called Chateau Gaillard which was designed by King Richard the Lionheart.

Most people, when they visit a castle, immediately ask: 'Where is the dungeon?' A good Castle Detective should be able to spot a dungeon without having to ask. But he should also know what sort of people were locked up and why.

At its simplest, a dungeon is a prison. To identify a prison, you must look for two clues. Both are very obvious, when you come to think about it. To lock people up, you need a lock or a bolt: and the bolt must be on the *outside* of the door. This is where the prison in a castle differs from all the other rooms. It is the only one with the bolt hole on the corridor side of the door jamb. Now you can see why it is so important to work out which way the doors in a castle opened. The prison door was the only one to open outwards into the corridor or guard-room.

Prisons had to be planned very carefully. The lord of the castle didn't want the prison next to his house. It tended to get rather smelly. He didn't want to hear the groans of the prisoners every time he went in or out. The prison had to be kept separate, somewhere where a guard could keep an eye on the prisoners. Since there was always somebody on duty at the gate-house, that was a good place for the prison.

Don't be misled, like most visitors, into thinking that every cold, dark room was a prison. Look for the clues at the doorway. Remember that many cold, dark rooms were for storage.

Not every castle had a prison, anyway. A prison is for criminals, people who have broken the law. If the lord of the castle was Sheriff of the county his job was to hold prisoners until they had been tried, and sometimes to keep them in prison afterwards if they were found guilty. He would need a proper prison, built for the purpose.

Not every lord kept criminals in his castle. Many kept prisoners of a different sort, however. If you could capture an enemy knight or baron during a battle you could hold him to ransom. It often took the relatives of the captured man some time to get the money to pay the ransom. A lord who was a successful fighter might have several captured knights in his castle while their ransoms were being arranged. These knights were not criminals. They had not broken the law. They might be as wealthy and important as the lord of the castle himself. It was no good locking them up in a cold, damp prison where they might fall ill and die. Who would pay ransom money for a dead man?

The richer the prisoner, the greater the ransom – and the more care you had to take to make sure he didn't die before the ransom was paid. Captured knights or barons were therefore well treated as a rule, provided they gave their word not to escape. They were treated almost as guests. No dark, damp 'dungeon' for them. If the lord of the castle

lived in a keep, they would live there with him. In the Middle Ages, no-one used the word 'dungeon'. They used the word *donjon*, but it meant a keep. It was only after the Middle Ages, when castles were abandoned and the old disused keeps were sometimes used to lock up criminals, that 'donjon' became 'dungeon' and was used to mean a prison.

Castles were thus not always grim fortresses, full of fierce knights and men-at-arms, with prisoners groaning in underground cells. Small or large, most of the time they were somebody's family home, with as many children living there as soldiers. Castles were built to look strong and fierce on the outside. On the inside they were made to look welcoming and comfortable. The grey stone walls were plastered or painted white. There were shutters at the windows. In the bailey there would be herb gardens for cooking and for medicine. There would be sounds of people talking, laughing or singing. There would be smells of cooking. The children who lived in the castle would be running all over it, playing games, creeping into the kitchen to see what was cooking, visiting the stables to see the horses, or the kennels to see the dogs. They might go fishing in the moat or in a nearby stream. They would have to work hard, too. Whatever they did, they were an important part of castle life.

The smells and the sounds have gone for ever. Herb gardens and window shutters leave little trace. Only the Castle Detective can spot the clues and work out what life in a castle was like. Only the Castle Detective can make sense out of what at first sight seems a meaningless jumble of walls and windows, fireplaces and doors. Without good detective work, the castles will keep their secrets locked within their walls. You can find the answers – if you try!

Check-list 4: How did they live in it?

Where are the houses in the castle?

Are they scattered about the bailey, or are they joined up to form
  ranges of buildings round a courtyard?

Can you find the Great Hall?

If there is a keep, the Great Hall may be there. But look to see if there is
  another later one.
Can you see two doors at the end of the Great Hall which lead to the
  pantry and buttery?

Where is the kitchen?

How many fireplaces and ovens are there?
How long would it have taken to carry food to the pantry and then into
  the Hall?
Can you find more than one kitchen. If you can, which part of the
  castle did the extra kitchen serve?

Where is the lord's apartment?

Can you find the lord's private hall? How does it compare with the
  Great Hall?
Can you find the lord's chamber? How warm and comfortable would
  it have been? Did it have a toilet?
How far is the lord's apartment from the kitchen? How would you
  have kept the food warm?

Where are the apartments for the guests?

How many separate apartments for guests can you find?
Are any of the apartments more comfortable than others?

Where is the chapel?

Is it built close to the lord's apartment?
Is there more than one chapel in the castle?
Does the chapel have a big window? If so, do you think it was a
    weakness in the castle's defences?

Where is the prison?

Can you find a room built specially as a prison? (Remember, not every
    castle had a proper prison.)
If a prisoner escaped from his prison, how easy would it have been for
    him to get out of the castle?

Chapter 5
Why is it empty?

This book has been written to help you explore a ruined castle. Have you ever wondered why a castle *is* a ruin? It's so easy to think of it as just a big adventure playground, full of secret stairs and passages. Some castles are so ruined that all the stonework has collapsed and become covered with earth and grass. In others, a whole town or modern factory covers the place where people lived or fought in the Middle Ages. Why? Where did all the people go?

In some ways, the fact that a castle is now a ruin is as remarkable as the fact that someone found it necessary to build it in the first place. In the Middle Ages barons and knights spent much of their money building castles. In fact they spent more money and time building castles than almost anything else. Yet in the end they went away and left them to fall into decay. Working out why this happened is one of the Castle Detective's hardest tasks.

First of all, why did the people stop building castles? Well, by the end of the Middle Ages a great many castles had been built. Few completely new ones can have been needed. All the same, this doesn't explain why people stopped re-building their castles to bring them up to date, as they had been doing for four hundred years since the Norman Conquest.

In Chapter 1 of this book we said that castles were built to protect knights. The main reason why men stopped building and re-building castles was that they had stopped being knights! This doesn't mean that important men stopped being called Sir This or Sir That, or that they stopped wearing swords. Men are still called Sir This or Sir That today, and army officers still wear swords on special occasions – but they aren't knights in the way that men were knights in the Middle Ages.

In the Middle Ages the king was supposed to give land – manor houses and estates – to his barons and knights on condition that they helped him rule the country. We have seen how he encouraged them to fortify their houses, so that they became castles, in order to have a number of safe places which his troops could use when necessary. We have also seen how useful these safe places were as court-rooms, customs posts, banks and armouries. All too often, however, his barons and knights fought against each other. Sometimes they even fought against the king! In other words, the system kept back-firing and damaging those it was intended to help. It was time for a different system.

Being a knight or baron was in any case becoming very expensive. As weapons became more and more effective, protection had to become more elaborate – and this meant both the metal armour which men wore on their bodies and the stone walls they built round their houses. Few people could afford the expense. The later Middle Ages also saw a number of battles which were won not by the wealthy knights and barons, but by armies of ordinary men using long-bows and pikes. This was very upsetting. What was the good of spending months or years learning to become a knight and buying an expensive horse and suit of armour, if some ordinary fellow could knock you off your horse with an arrow – or worse still, with a bullet?

Guns were just beginning to become effective at the end of the Middle Ages. At first they were small and unreliable. They tended to blow up and kill the gunners, and so were less use than a trebuchet or a cross-bow. But eventually guns became powerful enough to make a hole in a steel breast-plate or a stone wall. Guns didn't cause the end of castle-building by themselves, but they certainly made people think twice about spending a lot of money on castles.

These things may explain why people stopped building castles, but it doesn't explain why so many castles became empty. The change was a gradual one. The problem with designing a castle was this: you had to build a house that would be comfortable to live in all the time, but which would also be safe against attack on the few occasions when this was necessary. A really safe castle was usually uncomfortable to live in. So when there was a long period of peace, the lord of the castle would be tempted to enlarge the windows to let in more light. He might build an extra door at ground level to save having to go up a stairway to get into his old keep. As we have seen, many men had built what were really just comfortable houses disguised as strong castles. The walls were too thin, the windows too large, the moat too easy to drain, the machicoulations just for show. By the end of the fifteenth century, men gave up trying very hard to make their houses look like proper castles. Comfort came first. Some of the old ideas were still felt to be necessary. For example, the walls still had battlements, but the owner of the house didn't really expect to have to hide behind them while his archers fired at the enemy. There might be a moat, but if so it was largely for decoration, not to prevent tunnelling. Towers and turrets made the houses look cheerful instead of threatening.

The new fashion of the 16th century as displayed on royal palaces like Hampton Court, London. Notice the big windows which would be easy to attack.

When you visit a castle, look to see whether the last owner tried to make it more comfortable. Are there large windows with elaborate carved stonework inserted into towers built a hundred years or more before? Are there extra doors where no sensible castle defender would think of putting them? Look for the weak points in the castle defences. Try to work out whether they were the fault of the original designer, or of some later lord who put comfort before safety.

By the the sixteenth century, when the Middle Ages were at an end, most lords who had castles still lived in them occasionally. However, they spent most of their time in large houses which copied the new style of building favoured by the king. They wanted their houses to look like Hampton Court Palace, with big windows that showed how much expensive glass they could afford. Such windows would be no match for a trebuchet, let alone a cannon.

Sharp-angled earth ramparts have been added to the medieval defences of Carisbrooke Castle, Isle of Wight, to protect it against gunfire.

Cannon came to be the most feared weapons. Few castles could resist them. Even so, when civil war broke out in 1642 some castles were brought back into use. However to stand up to the cannon, a different style of fortification was needed. Earth ramparts were used to absorb the impact of the cannon balls. Such ramparts were usually built outside the castle walls, forming an outer ring of defence. Sharp-angled projections, called *bastions*, were added at the corners. Look carefully at each castle you visit to see if there are any signs of its having been re-fortified in this way during the seventeenth century.

By the beginning of the eighteenth century, most castles were abandoned and in ruins. Their stones were carried off to build new houses, cottages and pig sties! Lords and ladies demanded elegant houses, not mouldering piles of out-of-date stonework.

But, strangely enough, mouldering piles of out-of-date stonework

This 'castle' is really a fake. It was built in the 19th century to decorate the garden of a country house.

were just what people did want a hundred years later, in the nineteenth century. If you owned a large country mansion it became fahionable to have a ruined castle somewhere in your garden. If you weren't lucky enough to have a real one, you could always build a fake one! Britain suddenly sprouted imitation castles all over the place. These imitations, now usually called *follies*, were not very large – just an odd corner or two of wall, a broken tower perhaps. The builders didn't take much care to get them 'right', so if you look carefully you can always distinguish them from the real thing.

Not every castle is a ruin, however. Some are still lived in by their owners, though the present owners usually do not belong to the family that built the castle hundreds of years ago. Perhaps the most famous example of a castle which is still occupied is Windsor Castle, built by William the Conqueror soon after the Norman Conquest and still lived in by Her Majesty the Queen.

Other castles have remained in royal hands, even though they are not lived in by the Queen. When William the Conqueror captured Lincoln in 1068, he built a castle there to keep the local Saxon inhabitants in order. Anyone breaking the law was brought to trial in the Great Hall in the castle bailey. If you visit Lincoln Castle today, you will find that there is still a court-house in the bailey and that people are still tried there as they were nine hundred years ago. The Tower of London has also remained in royal hands: first as a castle, then as an armoury and prison, then as a mint for making coins. Now it is a tourist show-piece. But with its Crown Jewels, its soldiers to guard them, and its museum of armour, it still does part of the job it was built to do.

Other castles are entirely show-pieces. Although the owners may live in them, they have become far too expensive to keep up as private houses. In such cases the owner decides to open the castle to visitors. A guide may show you round and explain the castle's history to you. There may be exhibitions of armour and weapons. There may even be a souvenir shop and a restaurant.

Castles like these are very different from the castles we have been describing in this book. Each generation of owners since the Middle Ages will have altered the castle to make it more comfortable, turning it into a big country house surrounded by gardens. Many of the rooms will be furnished, though the furniture will usually have been made in the eighteenth and nineteenth centuries. It won't belong to the Middle Ages when the castle was built. Indeed, some of the more interesting looking bits of the castle itself may have been built only a hundred years ago.

Visiting a castle like this is very different from visiting a ruin. The castle is still somebody's house, so you cannot run, climb or hide in the way that you can if it is ruined. The detective work is more difficult too. Although the castle may look complete, much of what you see will not be medieval at all. Most of the original features – doorways, windows, battlements and garderobes – will have been replaced with modern stonework. This may not always copy the original stonework very closely.

Don't give up and follow the guide, just like everyone else. You have learned to use your eyes to discover clues as to how castles worked, which bits were built first, and how people lived in them. So as you go round, don't be distracted by all the more recent things. Look at them and enjoy them. They are almost always worth looking at. But keep on looking for the real bits of the old castle, hidden behind the modern furnishings. Look in the corners where visitors don't go as a rule. Look for old blocked-up windows and loops between the large airy windows put in more recently. Look for joins in the stonework where new buildings have been added to old ones. It's rather like looking at someone who is disguised and trying to work out what he really looks like underneath his false beard!

Arundel Castle, Sussex, has had large parts of it rebuilt in the 19th century. The Duke of Norfolk still lives there.

Corfe Castle, Dorset, has not been rebuilt. You must work things out for yourself here!

You will have to be careful how you do this. Don't make yourself so unpopular that you are asked to leave! A good detective doesn't let everyone know he or she is detecting. Just walk about quietly like everyone else, noticing things and storing them away in your mind. Fit them together like a jig-saw puzzle until you finally understand everything.

The best castles are those where you don't have to follow a guide, but can stay as long as you like in each part of the castle, visiting the various rooms in whichever order you please. But even if there is a guide, don't despair. Keep trying to work things out for yourself, then ask if you're right. Be careful to choose a good moment. Guides have to answer an awful lot of questions, so they sometimes get rather tired and cross. However, if they see that you are really interested, they will almost always do their best to help you. All guides are interested in their castles, and have to be Castle Detectives themselves to some extent. One detective should always help another!

Don't be disappointed if you don't get everything right at first, or if some castle defeats you every time you try. Even the best detectives have to admit defeat sometimes, if there aren't enough clues. The castle may be too ruined. It may be too rebuilt, too disguised by later wallpaper and furniture.

If this is the case, then relax and enjoy yourself. Give up detecting for a while. After all, what's the point of being a Castle Detective if you're not having fun!

How to make a model Castle

by Jasper Dimond

When you have read the rest of this book you will have a good idea of what the various parts of a castle were like, how they were used and who lived in them. A good way to help fix these essentials in your mind is to make a model, either on your own or with a grown-up to help you, or perhaps in class at school.

In the next few pages you will find instructions for making such a model. It isn't meant to be a model of any particular castle, but if you make it you will find that you can see much better why things in castles were the way they were.

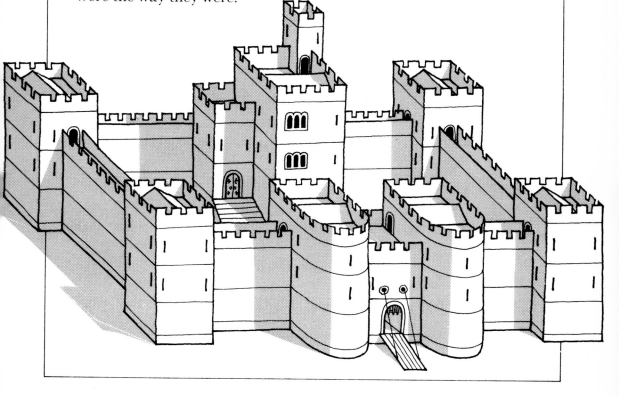

If you people it with toy soldiers (the dimensions given are suitable for 50 mm figures) you will be able to have a lot of fun thinking out for yourself all the ways of attacking and defending that were actually used in the old days, by playing siege games. (But remember to play fair – jumping on the model in a temper doesn't count!)

The first picture in this chapter is of a rather formal castle. It has a square bailey, with a keep in the middle, walls all round, with square wall-towers at the corners, and a gatehouse flanked by two 'D' towers in the middle of the front.

This is just to give you a basic idea; you needn't make your castle like this if you have other ideas. The model is made in separate pieces and you can put it together however you want, and even vary the size of it by making the walls longer or shorter. You can see one way of assembling it in the photograph on the back cover of this book.

You will need some thin cardboard or thick cartridge paper. The board known as ticket board is ideal, but almost any kind of thin board or stiff paper will do. You will also need some strongish glue. UHU is suitable, but use it sparingly. Another good glue is Evostik Woodworking PVA glue which comes in a squeezy bottle with a long nozzle.

You should read this chapter and look carefully at all the diagrams *before* you start, and not rush straight into making the gatehouse which is a bit more difficult – you'll only waste your time and cardboard.

Start with a square wall-tower. You will need several of these in any case, and in starting this way you will gain experience so that you are ready to tackle the more complex buildings.

Each of the buildings has been given its own section in the chapter, and there you will find special instructions for each building and also its overall dimensions.

Another section is given to details, and you should refer to this for laying out your battlements and so on.

In general, it is best to draw your doorways, arrow loops, windows, and so on, on a separate piece of paper, cutting them out and sticking them in position later, when you know exactly where you want them. Additionally, when you have finished your model, you could stick narrow strips of cardboard about 3 mm wide around your towers and walls to mark where the floors would be inside.

With very few exceptions, all the buildings are basically rectangular boxes and they are all made in the same general way. Each box has four equal rectangular sides plus a strip 25 mm wide down one edge with which to glue it together, a square ceiling panel with 25 mm strips round it, and a pitched roof panel. You should score the creases with the back of a blunt table knife along a straight edge on the wrong side before you fold them.

Try to be as accurate as you can when marking out and scoring; the more precisely you do this the more easily your buildings will fit together.

On two opposite sides of each tower are shown two upside-down 'U'-shaped cuts. The level flat parts of these cuts are on the edges on which the ceiling panel rests when it is slotted into position, so try and cut them exactly on the line of the ceiling. Get some help for this if necessary.

Alternatively, you might find it easier to put the ceiling in with the edge strips turned upwards and glue it in position lined up with the bottom edges of the crenels in the battlements, and you can do this if you prefer.

Keep

The Keep is a collection of rectangular buildings all glued together.

You will need a rectangle of card or paper 745 × 475 mm for the walls of the Keep; a rectangle 325 × 575 mm for the walls of the turret; and a rectangle 425 × 375 mm for the walls of the forebuilding. You will also need 6 rectangles of various smaller sizes for roofs and ceilings, and another piece about 231 × 300 mm from which to make the ramp up to the first floor level of the entrance in the forebuilding.

Notice that the battlements of the Keep are cut away to accommodate the turret in one corner, (of course you could put four turrets on if you wanted). The turret is slit up one corner from the bottom 425 mm up to the level of the ceiling of the Keep and two horizontal 55 mm cuts enable you to fold the side of the turret inwards to provide a glueing surface for attachment to the Keep tower.

The forebuilding is glued by one side to the side of the Keep tower and the ramp is glued in position on the Keep tower and forebuilding.

The ceilings and roofs are made to agree with the drawings. When they are glued in position, your Keep is complete and ready for painting.

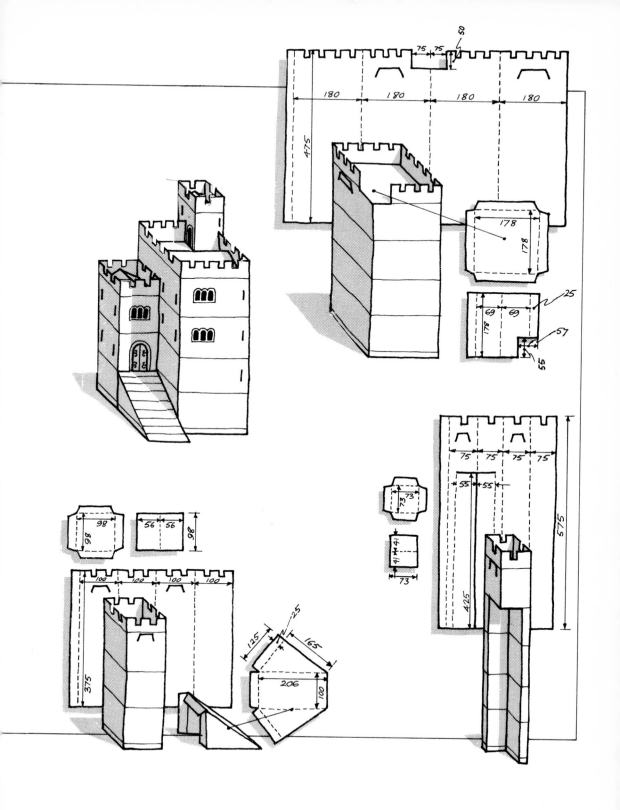

Square Wall Tower

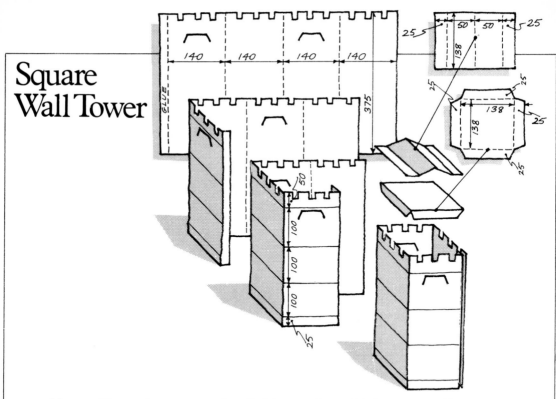

You will need a rectangle of thin card or thick paper 1625 mm × 375 mm and one piece 188 × 188 mm for the ceiling and another 150 × 138 mm for the roof.

Draw a line down one end of you large rectangle 25 mm from the edge to make a glueing tab, then draw three other lines at intervals of 140 mm. When scored and folded these will be the corners of your tower.

Next, lightly draw two lines across the top long side, one 25 mm down and the second 50 mm down, and lay out your battlements, centrally on each side of the tower.

Now carefully cut out the crenels with scissors.

Make your inverted 'U' cuts centrally in two opposite sides of your tower *before* you glue it up.

The ceiling and roof are made as shown in the drawings and once placed and glued in position your Square Wall-tower is complete except for painting.

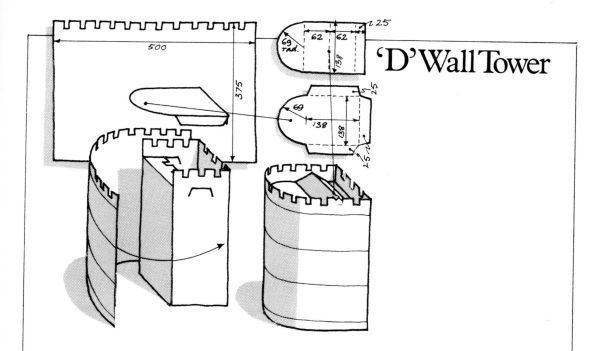

'D' Wall Tower

You will need a Square Wall-tower as described above, minus its ceiling and roof pieces, plus a rectangle of similar card or paper 500 × 375 mm for the rounded front and side walls, a piece 188 × 232 mm laid out with a rounded end and flaps as shown for the ceiling, and another piece 138 × 218 mm for the roof.

Make a slit 50 mm long down two adjacent corners of your square wall-tower and fold the battlements down inside as shown in the drawing to stiffen the top of this edge.

Cut your battlements along the top edge of the large rectangle and glue one end of it to one side of your tower.

Now curve your large rectangle round and glue the remaining end to the other side of the tower.

You may now insert and glue your ceiling and roof pieces in position and your 'D' tower is complete, ready for painting.

Gatehouse

The Gatehouse is a square tower with a tunnel through it, and is fitted with a drawbridge and a portcullis.

You will need a rectangle of card or paper 625 × 275 mm for the walls, another piece 350 × 150 mm for the tunnel, and three smaller pieces for roof, ceiling, and floor. You will also need two pieces of stiff cardboard, one for the drawbridge about 100 × 65 mm, and one from which to cut the portcullis, about 230 × 55 mm.

Make the walls of the Gatehouse in the same way as for the Square Wall-tower and cut out the battlements, arched doorways and holes for the drawbridge string, as shown in the drawings (you can cut the doorways in from the bottom edge because this will be held together when you glue the floor in place later). Glue together along the long corner flap.

Make your floor panel 150 mm square with 25 mm flaps all round.

Make the tunnel to the given dimensions and fold it as shown in the drawing (not forgetting to cut out the slot in its roof which should reach from side to side and be about 6 mm wide and about 15 mm from the front edge). Your portcullis will drop through this slot.

Paint the inside of your tunnel and the floor panel at this point – it will be nearly impossible later.

Glue the flat flaps of the tunnel in place on the floor panel. Then take the Gatehouse and, folding your four 'doors' inwards, carefully push the floor panel and tunnel into the bottom of the tower until it stops against the bottom edges of the doors. You can now carefully glue it in position.

Now you can make your ceiling panel. It is exactly the same as the floor panel, except that you have to cut a hole in it which coincides with the one in the tunnel roof (6 mm wide, 15 mm from the front fold edge and 45 mm from each side), so that the portcullis can drop straight down. Put it in position, but don't glue it yet.

The portcullis is made from your larger piece of stiff cardboard and should be cut to the shape shown in the drawing. (Don't worry about the flag and flagpole at this stage.) Get a grown-up to help here if necessary. When you have cut out your portcullis, check that it will drop freely through the slots in the ceiling and tunnel. If it falls satisfactorily you can glue the ceiling panel in place; if not you will have to see why, and adjust the hole in the ceiling as required.

Now you can cut out your roof panel and fold it ready for glueing. The hole in the roof is the same distance from the front edge as the others but is smaller, 6 × 25 mm, and placed exactly in the middle.

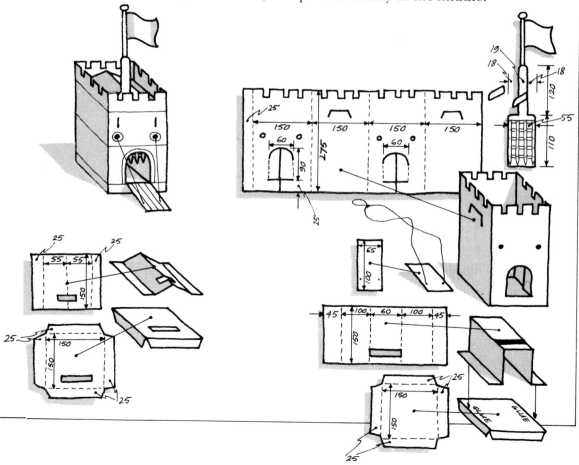

Place the portcullis in its slots in the 'down' position and try the roof in position. The tab on top of the portcullis should project through the hole in the roof by about 5 mm or so.

The catch on the portcullis is the next thing to make. Use a small piece of thick cardboard which is small enough to pass through the hole in the roof. Pull up your portcullis to a point where you can still see the bottom edge of it in the entrance to the tunnel, and make a mark on the long tab just where it emerges from the hole in the roof

Now remove the roof and portcullis and glue your small piece of cardboard into position with its *bottom* edge aligned with the mark you have just made on the tab. It should project to one side, making a sort of hook.

When the glue is set, you must draw and paint your portcullis on both sides. If you leave this until you have put the portcullis in position you will find it very difficult to do.

Once you have completed it and your glue and paint is dry you can drop it down through the ceiling and tunnel slots and pop the roof on over the long tab.

When you pull up the portcullis you should find you can just hook your catch over the edge of the roof hole to hold it up. By gently dislodging it with your finger, you can suddenly drop it again exactly like the real thing.

The drawbridge is hinged by sticky tape on the edge of the tunnel floor and drawn up by strings which pass through the holes provided and are tied together at the back of the Gatehouse.

Now glue the roof on. You can add your flag and pole now if you like.

Walls

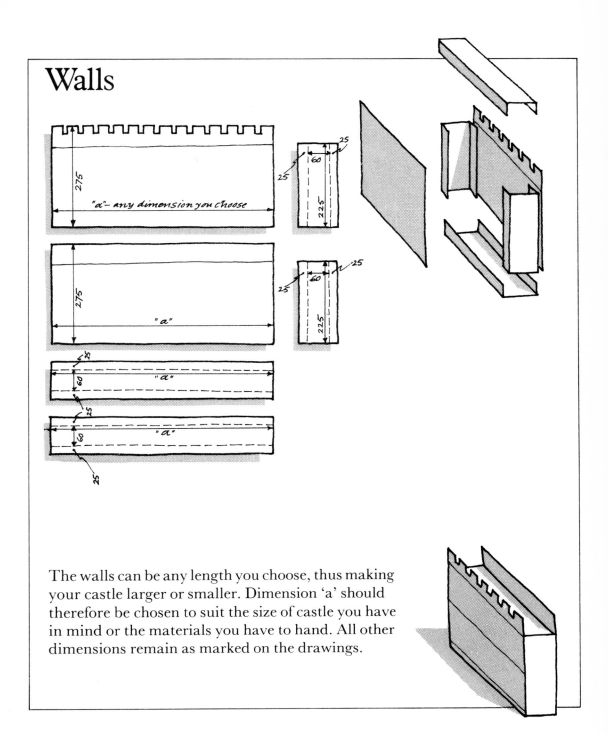

The walls can be any length you choose, thus making your castle larger or smaller. Dimension 'a' should therefore be chosen to suit the size of castle you have in mind or the materials you have to hand. All other dimensions remain as marked on the drawings.

Full-size Details

Details

You need not draw your doors, arrow-loops and windows exactly like this – you may have seen others which you would like to use – but remember to draw them about this size.

It is easiest to draw them on a separate piece of paper, cut them out and stick them in position when everything else is finished, and when you will know exactly where you want them.

The drawing showing the dimensions of your battlements also shows how the stonework might be laid out. You can colour your model using felt-tip markers or water-colours or poster-paints – almost anything you like. You could even cut out different-sized 'stones' in grey paper and stick them on.

It is best if the grey or stone colour you use for the stonework is not too dark.

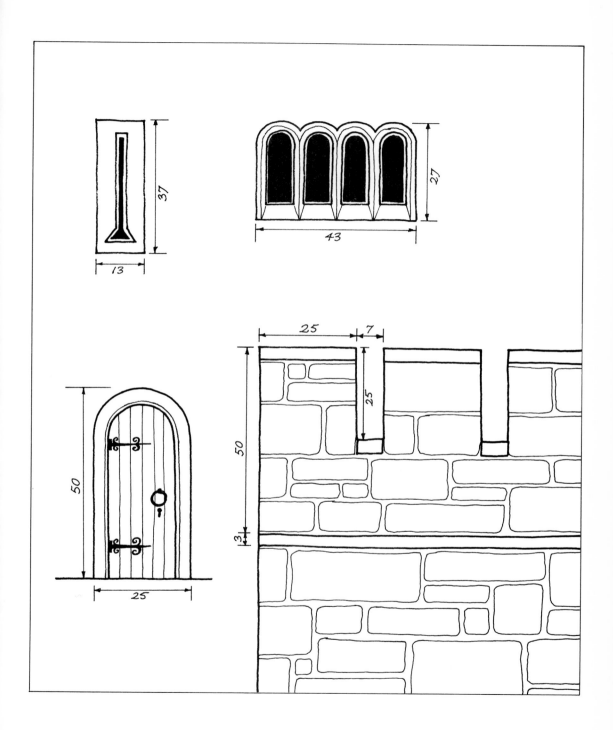

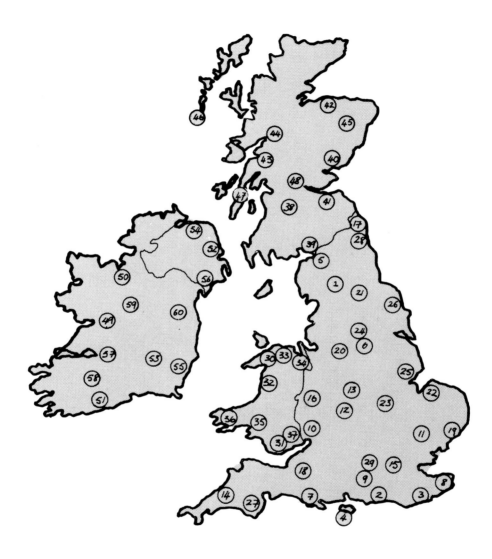

Castles you can visit

1. **Appleby**, *Cumbria (22km south-east of Penrith)*. This castle has two baileys. The inner bailey has a Norman keep. The wall-towers were added in the 13th and 15th centuries, and a large house was built in one of the baileys in the 17th century.

2. **Arundel**, *Sussex*. This was one of the first castles of the Norman Conquest. On top of the motte is a shell keep. The rest of the castle was almost entirely rebuilt in the 19th century, with huge towers and walls. But you can still see parts of the old castle bailey hidden in the 19th-century building if you look carefully.

3. **Bodiam**, *E. Sussex (19km north of Hastings)*. A square castle with round corner-towers and square gatehouses, set in a moat. It was built in AD 1385. The walls and towers are still complete, but the buildings inside have vanished.

4. **Carisbrooke**, *Isle of Wight*. A motte and bailey castle built on top of a Roman fort. There is a shell keep on top of the motte, a 13th-century gatehouse and a deep well worked by donkeys! In the 17th century extra defences were added against cannon.

5. **Carlisle**, *Cumbria*. A triangular castle set on a cliff in one corner of the town. There is a Norman keep and three gatehouses (one with a barbican). In the 16th century the castle was altered so as to withstand gunfire.

6. **Conisburgh**, *N. Yorkshire*. The oval bailey with its small rounded wall-towers encloses a magnificent round keep with six towers protruding from it. Outside the bailey gate is a barbican.

7. **Corfe**, *Dorset*. This enormous, sprawling castle is set high on a hill. In the inner bailey is a Norman keep. Early in the 13th century King John added a splendid new palace. The middle and outer baileys have round wall-towers; some of these were blown up by gunpowder during the 17th century.

8. **Dover**, *Kent*. A huge castle built on top of a prehistoric hill-fort, and enclosing a Roman lighthouse and a Saxon church. There is a Norman keep, two lines of defence with square and round wall-towers – and underground passages added in the 19th century.

9. **Farnham**, *Surrey*. The motte of this 12th-century castle was built round the lower part of a Norman keep. Later, the whole motte was enclosed in a shell keep. In the bailey are the buildings of the medieval Bishop's Palace.

10. **Goodrich**, *Herefordshire (8km south-west of Ross-on-Wye)*. A square castle with round corner-towers, gatehouse and barbican, built on a hill overlooking a ford. There is an outer line of defence on two sides. Inside there is a small Norman keep.

11. **Hedingham**, *Essex*. The bailey of this castle has lost all its stone walls and towers. But the Norman keep is very well preserved. It has five storeys, and gives a very good idea of what it was like to live in a castle in the 12th century.

12. **Kenilworth**, *Warwickshire*. The large outer bailey has wall-towers and a gate-house, protected by a lake. The inner bailey has a Norman keep and very elaborate accommodation added in the 14th century. The castle was brought up-to-date in the 16th century, when Queen Elizabeth I came to stay.

13. **Kirby Muxloe**, *Leicestershire*. This is one of the last castles to be built in England. It was still unfinished when building stopped in AD 1483. The rectangular moat, the gatehouse and a corner-tower still remain to show what the owner intended to build.

14. **Launceston**, *Cornwall*. A motte and bailey castle built to guard the road into Cornwall. On top of the very tall motte is a shell keep, and inside the shell keep is a round keep built early in the 13th century.

15. **London**, The Tower of London has buildings of almost every date. William the Conqueror's great keep stands at the centre, surrounded by two lines of defence with three gatehouses and a barbican. In the keep is a museum of arms and armour.

16. **Ludlow**, *Shropshire*. A great border castle, with two baileys. The walls and towers of both baileys are very well preserved, as is the gatehouse of the inner bailey. Inside the inner bailey is a most unusual chapel – it is round in plan.

17. **Norham**, *Northumberland (10km south-west of Berwick-on-Tweed)*. A border fortress, built to guard a ford across the river from Scotland into England. The Norman keep stands within defences rebuilt in the 15th and 16th centuries.

18. **Nunney**, *Somerset (8km south-west of Frome)*. A very tall keep, built in the French style in the later 14th century by an English knight who had made himself rich during the Hundred Years War between England and France. The keep was bombarded by cannon during the Civil War of the 17th century.

19. **Orford**, *Suffolk*. Only the keep remains of this royal castle built in the AD 1160's: but the keep is extremely well-preserved, and shows exactly how King Henry II thought a royal residence should be laid out.

20. **Peveril**, *Derbyshire (24km south-west of Sheffield)*. The triangular bailey is set on the edge of a high cliff. A Norman keep was built astride the bailey wall in about AD 1176. There are also the remains of a hall and chapel.

21. **Richmond**, *N. Yorkshire*. The large triangular bailey of this castle is set on a cliff above the river. The square wall-towers were an early experiment, and date from the 11th century. The early Norman gatehouse was turned into a keep in the 12th century.

22. **Rising**, *Norfolk (6km north-east of King's Lynn)*. The bailey of this castle is defended by enormous earth ramparts. Inside the bailey is a large, low Norman keep built as a comfortable and very impressive house. The keep walls have beautiful patterns carved on them.

23. **Rockingham**, *Northamptonshire (2km north of Corby)*. The motte of this motte and bailey castle was lowered to provide a platform for guns in the 17th century. The two baileys survive however. The 13th-century Great Hall is now part of a large house built in the 16th century.

24. **Sandal**, *W. Yorkshire*. This huge motte and bailey castle has only recently been excavated by archaeologists. On top of the motte are the ruins of a round keep, approached up a long defended stairway protected by a round barbican.

25. **Tattershall**, *Lincolnshire*. This rectangular castle, with its gatehouse and wall-towers, was originally built in the 13th century. In the middle of the 15th century a huge tower house was built to impress the neighbours. (If you look carefully you will see that some of the machicoulations are fakes!)

26. **Scarborough**, *N. Yorkshire*. The sea-cliff on which this castle stands was used by the Romans for one of their signal stations. Later the Normans built a square keep. In the bailey are the remains of two successive Great Halls. The bailey gate is protected by a barbican.

27. **Totnes**, *Devon*. A motte and bailey castle, built to guard the Saxon town of Totnes. On top of the tall motte is a shell-keep. Don't forget to look at the town walls and gatehouse!

28. **Warkworth**, *Northumberland*. This motte and bailey castle was built against Scottish raids over the border. The bailey walls and towers are well-preserved. In the later 14th century the Earl of Northumberland built a huge tower house on the motte. This has more rooms to explore than any other tower house or keep.

29. **Windsor**, *Berkshire*. The Queen still lives in this castle, originally built by William the Conqueror as a motte and bailey. All the buildings are complete, though some were rebuilt in the last century. Don't miss the beautiful Chapel of St George.

30. **Caernarvon**, *Gwynedd*. Built to establish English rule in Wales, this huge castle was never entirely finished. Even so, the walls and towers are complete and look very impressive. Beside the castle is the walled town of Caernarvon. You can follow the walls right round the town.

31. **Caerphilly**, *Glamorgan*. Begun in AD 1271, this enormous castle is surrounded by an artificial lake. Even the dam is defended! There are two lines of defence, four gatehouses and two barbicans.

32. **Castell Y Bere**, *Gwynedd*. A Welsh castle, built high on a mountain ridge in the 13th century. At each end of the long narrow bailey is a big round-ended tower. The bailey is protected by a barbican with its own gatehouse.

33. **Conway**, *Gwynedd*. Another big English royal castle. The high walls have eight huge round towers. Beside the castle is a town with walls and towers even more impressive than the town walls of Caernarvon.

34. **Flint**, *Clwyd*. This was one of the first big English royal castles to be built in Wales, a few years before Conway and Caernarvon. It is like a stone motte and bailey castle, with a round keep at one corner of the bailey instead of a motte. There was once an outer bailey, but his has almost disappeared.

35. **Kidwelly**, *Dyfed*. This rather unusual castle has a square inner bailey set within a semicircular outer bailey. It was built in the later 13th century, and has massive corner towers, a chapel tower, and a large gatehouse.

36. **Pembroke**, *Dyfed*. A baronial castle set on a peninsula jutting out into the sea. There are two baileys, each with wall-towers and a gatehouse. In the inner bailey is a large round keep. Underneath is a huge cave where the baron kept his boats!

37. **Raglan**, *Gwent (16km south-west of Monmouth)*. Built in AD 1461, this was one of the latest castles to be built. The bailey is divided into two courtyards. There is a large hexagonal keep, and a gatehouse with huge machicoulations. This was a castle meant to impress everyone who saw it.

38. **Bothwell**, *Strathclyde (13km south-east of Glasgow)*. The rectangular bailey has both round and square wall-towers. In one corner is a round keep. Outside are the traces of an unfinished outer bailey with round wall-towers and a gatehouse.

39. **Caerlaverock**, *Dumfries and Galloway*. A most unusual castle, built in the later 13th century and surrounded by a moat. The bailey is triangular and the towers have large machicoulations. Inside the bailey are later buildings of the 16th and 17th centuries.

40. **Claypotts**, *Tayside (5km east of Dundee)*. This tower house was built between AD 1569 and 1588. It has two round corner-towers attached at opposite sides. These towers have square turret-rooms on top of them, making the tower house look very dramatic.

41. **Craigmillar**, *Lothian (on the outskirts of Edinburgh)*. The walls of the bailey have machicoulations on them and the round corner-towers have gun-loops. The tower-house was built about fifty years earlier. Most of the domestic buildings were added in the 16th century.

42. **Duffus**, *Grampian (6km north of Elgin)*. A motte and bailey castle. There is a 14th-century keep on top of the motte, and 15th-century domestic buildings in the bailey.

43. **Dunstaffnage**, *Strathclyde (5km north-east of Oban)*. This 13th-century castle is set on a high rock. There is a rectangular bailey, with one corner-tower used as a keep. In the 17th century a tower house was built over the earlier entrance.

44. **Inverlochy**, *Highland (3km north-east of Fort William)*. This castle was built in the later 13th century. The square bailey has round wall-towers. One corner tower is larger than the others and was used as a keep.

45. **Kildrummy**, *Grampian (16km west of Alford)*. The first castle here was a motte and bailey. Later, in the 13th century, a new castle was built nearby with round wall-towers and a big gatehouse.

46. **Kiessimul**, *Isle of Barry*. This castle is built on a small island and is surrounded by the sea. It was probably built in the 13th century. There is a square keep of four storeys. The domestic buildings in the bailey were rebuilt in the 18th century.

47. **Skipness**, *Strathclyde (13km south-east of Tarbot)*. The late 13th-century bailey of this castle encloses an earlier 13th-century house of three storeys, and a chapel. In the 16th century a tower house was built in the bailey as well.

48. **Stirling**, *Central*. A Scottish royal castle built on a high rock. The Great Hall was built in the 15th century and has recently been restored. The palace buildings and royal chapel were added in the 16th century. In the 18th century the castle was taken over by the English army and many alterations were made.

49. Athenry, *Galway*. The rather irregular-shaped bailey has round corner-towers and was built in the 13th century. Inside is a square keep of three storeys.

50. Ballymote, *Sligo (22km south of Sligo town)*. A square castle, with round corner-towers and with square wall-towers between the corner-towers. It was built in the 13th century. The gatehouse has unfortunately been destroyed.

51. Blarney, *Cork*. The tower house which incorporates the famous Blarney Stone was built in the middle of the 15th century. Beside it is an earlier tower which is now used as an extra wing.

52. Carrickfergus, *Antrim*. A stern fortress built by the Normans soon after they arrived in Ulster. There is an inner bailey with a square keep, and an outer bailey with a 13th-century gatehouse. The castle was altered to withstand gunfire in the 16th century.

53. Clara, *Kilkenny (6km east of Kilkenny)*. A very well-preserved tower house built in the later 15th century. It has five storeys. There is a small courtyard or 'bawn'.

54. Dunluce, *Antrim (6km east of Portrush)*. This castle is magnificently set on a rocky crag at the edge of the sea. The castle was first built in the 13th century, the gatehouse was rebuilt in about AD 1600, and a large domestic house was added about 1640.

55. Ferns, *Wexford*. Only the keep of this 13th-century castle survives today. It is a very unusual keep, with big round corner towers attached to it, rather like Nunney Castle in Somerset.

56. Greencastle, *Down (10km south-west of Kilkeal)*. Near an old deserted motte is a large 13th-century castle with a rectangular bailey and rounded corner-towers. In the bailey is a rectangular keep built about AD 1260: it was heightened and altered in the 16th century.

57. Limerick, *Limerick*. This 13th-century castle, with its gatehouse and round corner-towers, was altered to withstand gunfire. The corner towers were lowered and a bastion was added in AD 1611. There is an 18th-century army barracks in the bailey.

58. Liscarroll, *Cork (11km north-west of Buttevant)*. This castle has a rectangular bailey with round corner-towers, a rectangular gatehouse and small square wall-towers along one side. It was built in the 13th century.

59. Roscommon, *Roscommon*. A four-sided castle was built here in the 13th century, with round corner-towers, a huge gatehouse and a postern tower. In AD 1580 new domestic buildings were added, and large windows were cut into the earlier defences.

60. Trim, *Meath*. The very unusual cross-shaped Norman keep is built on an old motte. The bailey is triangular and has open-backed wall-towers. The round postern tower has its own barbican tower.

There are a lot more castles than these. Look around near your home and see if you can find some of them.

Glossary

Assault A direct attack on a castle, using ladders to climb over the walls. Usually a very dangerous method of attack! See page 44.

Bailey The courtyard of a castle, where most of the domestic buildings (such as the hall, kitchen, chapel and storehouses) were. See pages 21–22.

Barbican An outer defence built to protect a gateway from direct attack. See page 50.

Barmkin A small courtyard or bailey attached to a *tower house* in northern England and Scotland. See page 35.

Baron An important knight who received his lands from the king rather than from another knight. See page 8.

Bastion A sharp-angled earth rampart used to protect a castle against guns. See page 91.

Battering-ram A large wooden beam or tree trunk, used to knock down walls and doors. Sometimes the end of the beam was carved to look like a ram's head. See page 44.

Battlements A row of square notches cut in a *parapet*. The notches are called *crenels* and the lengths of parapet between are called *merlons*. See pages 25–26.

Bawn The Irish name for the small courtyard or bailey attached to a *tower house*. See page 35.

Buttery The room next to the *hall* where drinks were prepared for serving. The butler was in charge of all the bottles. See page 73.

Cat A protective wooden shed, especially a shed over a *battering-ram*. It was used during a siege. See page 44.

Chamber A private room where the lord of the castle and his family, or their guests, could eat and sleep. See page 27.

Chapel A private church built for the special use of the lord of the castle. See page 27.

Constable A knight appointed to be in charge of a castle while the owner was away. See page 10.

Crenel A square notch cut in the *parapet* of a stone wall. The lengths of parapet between the crenels are called *merlons*. See pages 25–26.

Cross-bow A short powerful bow, sometimes made of metal, fixed to a wooden handle like a modern rifle or shotgun. More accurate than a longbow, but slower to use.

Donjon The medieval name for a *keep*. It is not a *dungeon*! See page 83.

Draw-bar A wooden beam which slides across the back of a door or gate to lock it shut. See page 53.

Drawbridge The removable part of a

bridge into a castle, making it difficult for an enemy to get close to the gates. See pages 51–52.

Dungeon An old name for an underground prison. Do not confuse with *donjon*! See pages 81–83.

Embrasure The large opening in the rear face of a wall behind a *loop*. (Some people also call *crenels* embrasures.) See pages 57–58.

Fief The land given to a knight in return for a promise to fight for the person who gave him the land. See page 8.

Folly An imitation ruin built during the 18th or 19th century to make a new garden look as though it had been there a long time. See page 92.

Forest Land, usually partly wooded, set aside for hunting so that it becomes a refuge for deer and wild boar.

Garrison A party of soldiers whose duty is to defend a castle. See page 44.

Hall A large room used for formal purposes, such as holding court, or for banquets. See page 71.

Garderobe A latrine or toilet, usually built in the thickness of the castle wall. See page 80.

Hourd A timber gallery or balcony fitted to a wall outside the battlements, with holes in the floor through which defenders could drop things on the enemy. See page 58.

Jamb The ridge at the side of a doorway against which the door shuts. See page 78.

Jousting A practice fight, in which a knight fought against a single opponent on horseback, using his lance to knock him off his horse.

Keep A large stone tower with thick walls. The rooms are arranged one above the other and the entrance is at first-floor level. Square keeps are older than round ones. See page 27.

Knight A warrior trained to fight on horseback with sword, spear and shield.

Long-bow An ordinary bow about 1·5–1·8m. long, held vertically when in use. Not as accurate as a cross-bow, but much quicker to use.

Loop A tall narrow opening designed to allow an archer to use his bow without being shot himself. See pages 57–58.

Machicoulation A row of holes in the underside of a projecting stone *parapet* through which things could be dropped on an enemy below. See page 62.

Mangonel A catapult for hurling stones. The arm of the catapult was worked by twisted ropes. See page 45.

Manor An estate (area of land) belonging to a lord or controlled by him.

Manor House The house where the lord of the manor lived and where his tenants came to pay their rent.

Mason A workman specially trained to carve stone and to build walls.

Merlon A length of stone parapet between two *crenels* (i.e. between two square notches cut in the *parapet*). See pages 25–26.

Mining Tunnelling under the walls of a castle so as to make them collapse. The best defence against mining was a *moat*. See page 47.

Moat A ditch dug round a castle and filled with water to prevent tunnelling. See page 38.

Motte A large artificial mound built to support a wooden tower. See page 20.

Mortar A mixture of lime, sand and water used to join stones together to make a wall.

Murder Holes Openings in the ceiling of a gate-passage through which missiles could be dropped or water poured to put out fires. See page 55.

Palisade A wooden wall made of up-right timbers, usually with a *sentry-walk* behind it. Often built on a *rampart*. See page 21.

Pantry The room next to the *hall* where food was prepared for serving. The panterer was in charge of the food. See page 73.

Parapet A stone screen on top of a wall, protecting a *sentry-walk*. Parapets were often notched to form *crenels*. See page 25.

Pike A very large pole with a spear-head on the end, used by foot-soldiers to keep horsemen away.

Piscina A small stone basin carved in the wall of a *chapel* near the altar, for washing the vessels used during a Mass. See page 76.

Portcullis A door that slides up and down on grooves, instead of opening and shutting on hinges. See page 53.

Postern A narrow gateway serving as a back door to a castle, easily defended because it is so narrow.

Rampart A protective barrier of earth, usually dug from a ditch and topped by a *palisade*. See page 21.

Sedilia A stone seat with an arch over it, carved in the wall of a *chapel* near the altar. See page 76.

Sentry-walk A pathway along the top of a wall, protected by a *parapet*. See page 25.

Shell keep A stone wall round the top of a *motte*, often replacing a wooden *palisade*. See page 24.

Sheriff An official appointed by the king to administer the law and to bring criminals to trial. See page 82.

Sow Another name for a protective shed used during a siege, especially a shed over a *battering-ram*. See page 44.

Steward An important servant responsible for looking after the domestic arrangements in a castle. See page 68.

Tournament A practice fight for groups of knights as a preparation for actual battle. Not to be confused with *jousting*.

Tower house A type of *keep* popular in the 14th and 15th centuries, especially in northern England, Scotland and Ireland. See page 35.

Trebuchet A large catapult for hurling stones. It was more effective than a *mangonel*, since it used counterweights instead of twisted ropes. See page 46.

Vault A stone ceiling or roof. Vaults may be rounded like a barrel or pointed. Rounded vaults are usually older than pointed ones. See page 37.

Wall-tower A tower built astride a castle wall so that archers can fire along the face of the wall. Wall-towers may be square or round in plan. As a rule, square wall-towers are older than round ones. See pages 30–31.

Windlass A machine for winding up the ropes of a *portcullis*. See page 53.

Window-seat A stone seat built into the side of a large window so that the person sitting there could see out. See page 71.

Index